PERGAMON GENERAL PSYCHOLOGY SERIES

Editors: Arnold P. Goldstein, *Syracuse University*
Leonard Krasner, *SUNY, Stony Brook*

Existential Man

The Challenge of Psychotherapy

PGPS-8

Existential Man

The Challenge of Psychotherapy

by

RICHARD E. JOHNSON, Ph.D.

*Associate Professor of Psychology and
Director of Clinical Training
University of Saskatchewan
Regina, Sask., Canada*

with
an Introduction by
JOHN WARKENTIN, Ph.D., M.D.,

*Editor of VOICES, The Journal of the
American Academy of Psychotherapists
Atlanta, Ga., U.S.A.*

PERGAMON PRESS

New York ● Toronto ● Oxford ● Sydney ● Braunschweig

PERGAMON PRESS INC.
Maxwell House, Fairview Park, Elmsford, N.Y. 10523

PERGAMON OF CANADA LTD.
207 Queen's Quay West, Toronto 117, Ontario

PERGAMON PRESS LTD.
Headington Hill Hall, Oxford

PERGAMON PRESS (AUST.) PTY. LTD.
Rushcutters Bay, Sydney, N.S.W.

VIEWEG & SOHN GmbH
Burgplatz 1, Braunschweig

Printed in the United States of America

08 016325 4

Contents

Introduction

I recommend this book to those of you interested in psychotherapy. It has made a meaningful contribution to my professional development, and offers pathways toward further emotional growth to any thoughtful person. However, Dr. Johnson does require that the reader be willing to set aside the conventional medical model of paternalistic evaluation and advice. He asks us to shift over to an emphasis on the mutual relating of persons, rather than the "sick" one leaning on the professional wisdom of the "doctor." The only "mental illness" is estrangement from the Self and from others; the "cure" is active encountering with a human mediator. The author is highly disciplined, and expects the same of those who would sincerely seek growth in personal stature. He has little sympathy for status-seekers, comfort-seekers, or parent-seekers. *Existential Man* describes clearly the qualities of human encounters which can lead to new personal freedom and nobility for people who refuse to live constipated lives.

Dr. Johnson is constructively rebellious. He does not offer another school of therapy or system of treatment. He is not competing with physicians, nor does he even want to be a physician of the soul. By not diagnosing illness in people, he proceeds promptly to a non-healing kind of effort: A primitive, mutually sharing, and almost brutally honest relating with whatever Significant Other is present at the moment. In such relating the therapist is a hireling of the Other, accompanying this Other in the exploring of new paths to walk. This is so very different from hallowed Hippocratic tradition in which the wise physician appears almost like a God who tells people what to do and where to go. Dr. Johnson does use his extensive knowledge of psychopathology, psychophysiology, and psychodynamics, but only to facilitate his approach in such a way that the Other might find him to be an acceptable companion.

Existential Man reminded me of the writings of Georg Groddeck, John N. Rosen, Robert C. Murphy, Jr., Alexander Lowen, and other pioneers. Dr. Johnson appears on each page with clear transparency. The book is not calculated. We are invited to open this work on any page. The writing is lively and readable, and I was pleased to see that Dr. Johnson is fond of elephants. Maintaining my interest with his rapid pace, he moves from thoughtful quotations to verbatim dialogues between client and therapist to brief summaries outlining the critical commitment, congruent encounter, and existential ground of a journey with an Other.

My feeling approves the opinion that it is better to exist than just be happy on our journey, and we will do well to kill the kind of God who serves as a comfort station. We must seek bridges along the path toward existing ever more freely, with a willingness to risk our Selves in the venture of becoming. Man has a choice of cultivating a comfortable distance from others, or seeking encounters with others; pain as well as joy will be the portion of those who reach into an Other. The process of becoming is so difficult that "there can be no arbitrary restrictions on the modes of congruent participation." Dr. Johnson pushes such empathic involvement to its limits and beyond. "The therapist who will not touch a client with his body will not touch a client at all." This is indeed a severe attack on established and respected psychology shopkeepers. But it is even more a sharing of the author's seeking of experience and his joy that the mystery of human nature escapes our probing and thus remains inviolate.

John Warkentin, Ph.D., M.D.

Preface

Today psychology is being transformed from within by processes of evolution and revolution. Its basic assumptions have been challenged by such respected thinkers as Rogers, Maslow, May, Bugental—and the list grows longer. Still, as yet, such work has had relatively little impact on the field of psychology as a *whole*. The psychotherapist who tries to function within the confines of structured psychological institutions soon encounters this deeper resistance to existentialism. He soon discovers that the excitement generated by existential study is circumscribed and cannot assuage the pain of his own immediate aloneness. He is still told in the routine of his own professional world that he must "do the job of a psychologist as *we* define it or *get out!*" *Existential Man* was written under the pressure of such institutional attitudes and it reflects the conflict, anger, and rebellion inherent in the development of a complex field. I am convinced from my own assessment of contemporary psychology that this will be the stance required of "existential man" for a protracted time to come. Even a longer list of pioneers will not ease his burden—only one alone encounters existence and each of us must be that "one."

My own struggle with existence began as an undergraduate student twenty years ago. I was a client in psychotherapy and experienced a crisis which opened me to a new world of possibility. The initial breakthrough was followed by a series of critical encounters which spanned several years of my life. It was during these crucial years of self-discovery that psychotherapy and existence became meaningful to me as a person and as a psychologist. I "followed myself" through these exploratory years to my own "brand" of existentialism and tried to develop a therapeutic method by which it could be implemented. I later worked under Dr. Carl Rogers at the Psychiatric Institute of the University of Wisconsin and the Western Behavioral Sciences Institute in Southern California. The interaction with Rogers was invaluable as a means of sorting out the similarities and differences between my own existential method and the client-centered approach. These last years of theoretical organization and therapeutic practice have been essential to my development as a psychotherapist. Yet I *became* a psychotherapist during those critical years when I was a client in search of myself. I humbly acknowledge my indebtedness to those persons who supported me during the earlier years of personal crisis and encouraged me during the later years of professional development.

The work presented here is a condensation of these twenty years as student, client, and therapist. I wrote in a manner dictated by the nature of the work itself. I wrote *Existential Man* in the mood of a practicing psychotherapist and not in the style of a scholar. It was not my intention to make it fit the system. The text itself does not contain a bibliography. The primary references are to my own experiences and those of my clients. Even the references to existentialism have more personal than theoretical significance. The explicit purpose of the book is to present these personal experiences and a conceptual organization of them. The implicit purpose of the book is to present a therapist's impression of existential man. I use critical encounters in psychotherapy as the figure and set that figure against the ground of existentialism. The existential ground then points beyond itself toward an infinite horizon into which each one is free to venture as far as he will choose.

R.E.J.

Acknowledgments

Grateful acknowledgment is made to the following publishers for permission to reprint selections from the works listed:

Harper & Row Publishers, Inc., New York, *The Meaning of the Creative Act* by Nicolas Berdyaev, trans. by Donald A. Lowrie © 1962; *Solitude and Society* by Nicolas Berdyaev, trans. by Donald A. Lowrie © 1965; and *Being and Having* by Gabriel Marcel © 1965.

Dacre Press, A & C Black Ltd., London, for *Being and Having* by Gabriel Marcel © 1949.

Alfred A. Knopf, Inc., New York, for *The Myth of Sisyphus* by Albert Camus, trans. by Justin O'Brian © 1955; and *The Rebel* by Albert Camus, trans. by Anthony Bower © 1956.

Librarie Gallimard, Hamish Hamilton, London, for *The Rebel* by Albert Camus, trans. by Anthony Bower © 1951.

The Macmillan Co., New York, for *Notes from the Underground* by Fyodor Dostoevsky, trans. by Constance Garnett © 1952, and *Between Man and Man* by Martin Buber, trans. by Ronald Gregor Smith © 1960.

William Heinemann Ltd., London, for *Notes from the Underground* by Fyodor Dostoevsky, trans. by Constance Garnett © 1956.

Routledge and Kegan Paul Ltd., London, for *Between Man and Man* by Martin Buber, trans. by Ronald Gregor Smith © 1947.

The Philosophical Library Inc., New York, for *The Emotions* by Jean-Paul Sartre, trans. by Bernard Frechtman © 1948.

Princeton University Press, New Jersey, for *The Concept of Dread* by Soren Kierkegaard, trans. by Walter Lowrie (copyright 1944, © 1957 by Princeton University Press; Princeton Paperbacks, 1967): reprinted by permission of Princeton University Press, and *Concluding Unscientific Postscript* by Soren Kierkegaard, trans. by David Swenson and Walter Lowrie (copyright 1941, © 1969 by Princeton University Press; Princeton Paperback, 1968): reprinted by permission of Princeton University Press and the American Scandinavian Foundation.

Charles Scribner's Sons, New York, for *Slavery and Freedom* by Nicolas Berdyaev, trans. by R. M. French © 1941, and *I and Thou* by Martin Buber, trans. by Ronald Gregor Smith © 1958.

Voices, John Warkentin, Editor, for selections first published as "Limits and Cornerstones" (Vol. IV, No. 3 © 1968), "The Therapeutic Imperative" (Vol. II, No. 2 © 1966), and "The Critical Commitment" (Vol. II, No. 1 © 1966) by Richard E. Johnson.

Existential Man

The Challenge of Psychotherapy

The physician in an insane asylum who is foolish enough to believe that he is wise for all eternity and that his bit of reason is insured against all injury in life is indeed in a certain sense wiser than the crazy patients, but at the same time he is more foolish, and he surely will not heal many.

Kierkegaard, *The Concept of Dread.*

Part I

Foundations

Chapter 1
The Critical Commitment

I am a psychologist. Yet I hate psychology. I owe it no allegiance. It has only abused me and those values most important to me. I was expelled from one department because "you have personality problems that will interfere with your development as a psychologist." I was then refused admission to most other departments because "you do not have the attributes of a psychologist." The department that did grant me a degree tried to expel me even after a completed dissertation because "you do not think in the mainstream of psychology." I rebelled in defense of subjective man and was repeatedly punished for it. Psychology studied the facade of man. I wanted to study man himself. My commitment to subjective existence was rejected as either naïve or pathological. My discontent with psychology was dismissed as either personal or professional failure. I will not forget the vindictive reaction of psychology to me.

Alienation from psychology drove me deeper into my own solitude. I had been alone often in the past. Most of life was alien to me. I hated every organized intellectual and social system. I hated most the systems of psychology. I asserted myself against these calculated answers to existence. I spurned these logical reductions of man. I explored my deepest subjective self to discover a more vital reality. That subjective search led me into lonely solitude. I risked it then. I risk it now.[1]

The solitude did become dangerously morbid. I began to fear emotional isolation from other men. I began to feel cut off from life itself. Panic attacks were now accompanied by glimpses and threats of more severe disorganization. The anxiety I once controlled now overwhelmed me. Yet the intensity of that personal crisis was the occasion for a vital encounter with myself. The self I discovered was not the effigy of man made by psychology. The man they made is determined. I choose my own destiny.

I will not argue for the reality of metaphysical propositions. I am indifferent to logical pros and cons. I know only what is real for me. I know that the assumption of habitual behavior breaks

---

[1] I do not want to be misunderstood. So do I hate psychiatry and social sciences other than psychology. Each is dominated by reductive systems which destroy the existential reality of man.

down under stress. Nothing repeats itself as a function of the past.
There is no repetition. Each moment is a critical challenge. I meet
that challenge by intentional choice and voluntary action or I cease
to exist. Each moment demands of me the labor of my own will.
Habitual repetition is the illusion. Freedom is the existential reality.

Yet for psychology freedom is the illusion. It plans even now an
"illusion of freedom" for future man. It will fail as must every
illusion. To act is not to be. The distinction between the feigned
and the real is categorical. To act Socrates is not to be Socrates. To
act suicidal is not to be suicidal. The cup was fatal only to Socrates.
The actor will play the part many times again.

So to act free is not to be free. The actor flounders between the
feigned and the real. He cannot exit by an encounter with the feigned.
An encounter with the psychological model would destroy the illusion.
He cannot exit by an encounter with the real. He can be free no
more than he was suicidal. It is all pretense. It is a partial world of
stage illusion. I reject such a burlesque of life. I choose an encounter
with the real world. I choose the reality of existential freedom.

The audience may fail to distinguish Socrates from an impersonator of Socrates. Observation is fallible. Socrates and the impersonator
would know. An illusion breaks against the reality of the phenomen
itself.

Let times so change that only one alone still cares. I will be that
"one."

The Existential Ground

on primordial freedom

Dostoevsky: Notes from the Underground

"Ha! ha! ha! But you know there is no such thing as choice in reality,
say what you like," you will interpose with a chuckle. "Science has
succeeded in so far analyzing man that we know already that choice
and what is called freedom of will is nothing else than _____"

Stay, gentlemen, I meant to begin with that myself. I confess, I was
rather frightened. I was just going to say that the devil only knows what
choice depends on, and that perhaps that was a very good thing, but
I remembered the teaching of science . . . and pulled myself up. And
here you have begun upon it. Indeed, if there really is some day discovered a formula for all our desires and caprices—that is, an explanation
of what they depend upon, by what laws they arise, how they develop,
what they are aiming at in one case and in another and so on, that is a
real mathematical formula—then, most likely, man will at once cease
to feel desire, indeed, he will be certain to. For who would want to
choose by rule? Besides, he will at once be transformed from a human
being into an organ-stop or something of the sort; for what is a man
without desires, without free will and without choice, if not a stop in
an organ? . . .

But . . . the stone wall! What stone wall? Why, of course, the laws of nature, the deductions of natural science, mathematics. As soon as they prove to you, for instance, that you are descended from a monkey, then it is no use scowling; accept it for a fact. When they prove to you that in reality one drop of your own fat must be dearer to you than a hundred thousand of your fellow-creatures, and that this conclusion is the final solution of all so-called virtues and duties and all such prejudices and fancies, then you have just to accept it; there is no help for it, for twice two is a law of mathematics. Just try refuting it.

"Upon my word," they will shout at you, "it is no use protesting: it is a case of twice two makes four! Nature does not ask your permission, she has nothing to do with your wishes, and whether you like her laws or dislike them, you are bound to accept her as she is, and consequently all her conclusions. A wall, you see, is a wall . . . and so on, and so on." Merciful Heavens! but what do I care for the laws of nature and arithmetic, when, for some reason, I dislike those laws and the fact that twice two makes four? . . .

Now I ask you: What can be expected of man since he is a being endowed with such strange qualities? Shower upon him every earthly blessing, drown him in a sea of happiness, so that nothing but bubbles of bliss can be seen on the surface; give him economic prosperity, such that he should have nothing else to do but sleep, eat cakes and busy himself with the continuation of his species, and even then out of sheer ingratitude, sheer spite, man would play you some nasty trick. He would even risk his cakes and would deliberately desire the most fatal rubbish, the most uneconomical absurdity, simply to introduce into all this positive good sense his fatal fantastic element. It is just his fantastic dreams, his vulgar folly that he will desire to retain, simply in order to prove to himself—as though that were so necessary—that men still are men and not the keys of a piano, which the laws of nature threaten to control so completely that soon one will be able to desire nothing but by the calendar. And that is not all: even if man really were nothing but a piano-key, even if this were proved to him by natural science and mathematics, even then he would not become reasonable, but would purposely do something perverse out of simple ingratitude, simply to gain his point. And if he does not find means he will contrive destruction and chaos, will contrive sufferings of all sorts, only to gain his point! He will launch a curse upon the world, and as only man can curse (it is his privilege, the primary distinction between him and other animals), maybe by his curse alone he will attain his object— that is, convince himself that he is a man and not a piano-key! If you say that all this, too, can be calculated and tabulated—chaos and darkness and curses, so that the mere possibility of calculating it all beforehand would stop it all, and reason would reassert itself, then man would purposely go mad in order to be rid of reason and gain his point! I believe in it, I answer for it! . . .

You will scream at me (that is, if you condescend to do so) that no one is touching my free will, that all they are concerned with is that my will should of itself, of its own free will, coincide with my own normal interests, with the laws of nature and arithmetic. Good Heavens, gentlemen, what sort of free will is left when we come to tabulation and arithmetic, when it will all be a case of twice two makes four? Twice two makes four without my will. As if free will meant that!

Berdyaev: The Meaning of the Creative Act

Creativity is inseparable from freedom. Only he who is free creates. Out of necessity can be born only evolution; creativity is born of liberty. When we speak in our imperfect human language about creativity out of nothing, we are really speaking of creativity out of freedom. Viewed from the standpoint of determinism, freedom is "nothing," it surpasses all fixed or determined orders, it is conditioned by nothing else; and what is born of freedom does not derive from previously existing causes, from "something." Human creativity out of "nothing" does not mean the absence of resistant material but only an absolute increment or gain which is not determined by anything else. Only evolution is determined: creativity derives from nothing which precedes it. Creativity is inexplicable: creativity is the mystery of freedom. The mystery of freedom is immeasurably deep and inexplicable. Just as deep and inexplicable is the mystery of creativity. Those who would deny the possibility of creation (creativity) out of nothing must inevitably place creativity in a certain determined order and by this very fact must deny the freedom of creativity. In creative freedom there is an inexplicable and mysterious power to create out of nothing, undetermined, adding energy to the existing circulation of energy in the world. As regards the data of the world and the closed circle of the world's energy, the act of creative freedom breaks out of the determined chain of the world's energy. From the viewpoint of an immanent world datum this act must always represent creation out of nothing. The timid denial of creation out of nothing is submission to determinism, obedience to necessity. Creativity is something which proceeds from within, out of immeasurable and inexplicable depths, not from without, not from the world's necessity. The very desire to make the creative act understandable, to find a basis for it, is failure to comprehend it. To comprehend the creative act means to recognize that it is inexplicable and without foundation. The desire to rationalize creativity is related to the desire to rationalize freedom. Those who recognize freedom and do not desire determinism have also tried to rationalize freedom. But a rationalization of freedom is itself determinism, since this denies the boundless mystery of freedom. Freedom is the ultimate: it cannot be derived from anything; it cannot be made the equivalent of anything. Freedom is the baseless foundation of being: it is deeper than all being. We cannot penetrate to a rationally-perceived base for freedom. Freedom is a well of immeasurable depth—its bottom is the final mystery.

Chapter 2
The Existential Self

My life has been criticized as a "preparation for Hell." I am told by these critics that "Heaven is just around the corner." Such prophecies of Utopia are made by both the right and left in psychology. Those on the right argue that I need my "behavior modified." Those on the left recommend that I have my "mind blown." The former can be done by application of the correct social "program." The latter can be done by drugs and "sensitivity" games. These two contradictory trends in contemporary psychological theory agree on one point: my condition is critical. Each offers a cure. I have given their diagnoses and suggested remedies careful consideration. I choose the "sickness" of existence.

Nicolas Berdyaev predicted a utopian renaissance in his *The Meaning of the Creative Act*. The book was written in 1911. It was published in 1927. Many critical events occurred during those intervening years. These were events which shook the foundations of history. So did they topple Berdyaev's dream of Utopia. He added an introductory note to the 1927 publication. It summed up the change in his perspective: "A new epoch in history has begun. The bases of my thinking remain unaltered. In my book, I gave warning that the old world was going to pieces. But now the definiteness of my book appears to me as too optimistic. My faith in the imminent dawn of a creative religious epoch was too great. The book was written in one single movement, and it reflects the 'Sturm und Drang' period of my life. Today I am inclined to greater pessimism, and this is expressed in my *The Meaning of History*."

This pessimism concerning social change did not alter Berdyaev's optimism about man himself. He did not recant his basic faith in the creative religious spirit. Berdyaev remained a "Russian boy" until his death in 1948 at the age of 73. I cite his response because I respect both the depth of his understanding and the breadth of his experience. He wrote this qualifying note direct from critical involvement at the vortex of historic social change. His struggle for freedom resulted in exile to Siberia by Czarist Russia before the revolution. He was then exiled again after the revolution by the Bolshevik government. The freedom which he demanded was deeper than political change. I cite Berdyaev's personal reaction for another reason as well. I want to use his thinking as a point of departure to explain my own "preparation

5

for Hell" and my own rejection of contemporary proposals for "Heaven on earth."

Berdyaev was a Christian philosopher but his concept of man goes much deeper. He was committed to the creative spirit in man which transcends any particular religion and yet, at the same time, is imbedded in each of them. It is my plan to circumvent religions in order to deal directly with this underlying metaphysics of the human condition. Consequently, we can use the conceptual terminology of religious existentialists aware that our only concern is the spiritual nature of man in its pristine form.

Berdyaev divided human evolution into three epochs. These stages paralleled the Triune Deity of God the Father, Son, and Holy Ghost. Man must pass through these three phases of history to attain his ultimate consummation. The epochs were coexistent and resisted the establishment of definite chronological limits. He felt that man had not fully outlived the law (the Father); redemption from sin (the Son) was not yet completed; still man was on the verge of the spiritual epoch (the Holy Ghost). It was his pessimism concerning the imminence of this spiritual epoch that he expressed in 1927: "The crisis through which humanity is passing offers no hope for the possibility of an immediate move into religious creativity." Man was not yet ready for the transition from human pain to divine joy. Heaven was still a long way off. I must now leave Berdyaev and explain my own pessimism about modern formulas for an "instant Heaven."

No one can refute the fact that ethical mores are being transformed by scientific advances in medicine and technology. The traditional ethics of physical pain and physical labor have become historically obsolete. They no longer determine the character of culture and of man. Yet the crisis in human evolution has not been precipitated by this ethical transformation. Nor has it been precipitated by scientific breakthroughs in artificial contraception, in artificial transplantation, even in artificial life itself. The clamor over these issues is but "sounding brass." The *critical* danger to man is that these same scientific instruments are being used to cut out his psychological heart. They are being used by modern prophets to eliminate psychological pain and psychological labor. Man cannot survive such surgery at this stage of human evolution. Pain and labor generate dynamic energy for man's commitment to his metaphysical self. They are life blood to the contemporary epoch of "redemption." Cut these vital forces out of man with manipulation, drugs, or games and he will surely die.

I want to describe more succinctly the significance of pain and labor at this crucial stage of human evolution. Man dwells within two existential worlds at the same time. One is the solitary world of his intrapsychic life. The other is the social world of his interpersonal life. The latter world is superimposed upon the former and a state of tension exists within and between the two worlds. It is these tension states which make pain and labor necessary. The modern prophets of Utopia consider these states pathological. They are equally blunt in their explanation of my personal pathology: "You are alienated from yourself and that explains your tension." They prescribe the "cure" of "harmonious balance" at the center of a wholistic environment. Such a balance eliminates tension and liberates man. But freedom is not a balanced state for me. Freedom tears at my existential guts. I reject the balanced neutrality of a "both/and" solution. Only the pain of "either/or" cuts a growing edge. I want to focus on this growing edge in the primary existential relationship of man with himself.

I begin with a rejection of the common assumption that human motivation is biological, sociological, or psychological. I reject the assumption that man is determined by the "facts" of biology, sociology, or psychology. I argue rather that human motivation and human evolution are directed by a psychic energy that is metaphysical. The term *metaphysics* must be introduced because the origins of this psychic energy cannot be determined. The energy is an existential given. It emerged from that enigmatic period of evolution when consciousness became aware of itself and that awareness of the self became the decisive human factor. Then the existence of the self, rather than biological survival, began to direct the destiny of man.

Such a concept of metaphysical motivation is not just a bizarre whim of my own as it has often been labeled. The struggle to encounter and define this psychic energy has occupied philosophers and theologians across cultures and across time. This same struggle to encounter the metaphysics of the self underlies the labored efforts of contemporary existential thinkers. My goal in psychotherapy is to engage each individual client in a personal struggle to encounter the existential self within him.

Clients present themselves for psychotherapy because they suffer from pathological anxiety and guilt. It is pathological because it is a reaction to the obsolete epoch of socialization by authority. I am in agreement with both the right and the left that "God is dead." It is precisely because of this advance in evolution that I reject proposals from the psychological right. Behaviorism and psychoanalysis are steps backward since they only substitute another "program" or "system" of authority for the obsolete authority of God. So do proposals from the psychological left threaten to destroy this progress in human evolution. They recommend shortcuts to the "divine" which vitiate the very means by which an authentic reconciliation between man and "God" might ultimately be achieved. It is for these reasons that I refuse to offer clients any "cure" of relief from the pain and labor of anxiety and guilt. Instead, I bend my being like a contortionist to engage the client in an existential crisis that will precipitate an intrapsychic metamorphosis. The crisis will transform these pathological symptoms into existential drives: i.e., the energy invested in the obsolete struggle with an authoritarian God will be directed forward toward reconciliation with the spirit of "God." The dynamics of socialization will be destroyed and from that process of destruction the existential self will emerge.

The crisis which generates this metamorphosis is precipitated by the client's encounter with pathological anxiety and guilt. The dynamics of this crisis[1] mobilize resources within the client which enable him to master the presenting pathology of socialization. The client struggles through encounter with this pathology, but Heaven is not "just around the corner." It is not enough to kill God. Those who rejoice over his death and enter the Kingdom of Heaven may produce a Hell in human evolution from which there is no return. The clients I consider cured do not rejoice. They do not boast of "balanced liberation." They know their painful struggle with existence has just begun. They realize that now they bear a greater anxiety and a greater guilt than before they began psychotherapy. Yet these ills are not pathological. They are not a reaction to the obsolete epoch of socialization by authority. Those ills were destroyed as God the Father was killed in psychotherapy. The sickness with which they are now afflicted is inherent in the human condition at this stage of evolution. It is not a reaction to the past, but a demand of the present in a hope for the future.

This demand is an onerous one. We rejoice over the destruction of authority, but the joy is transient. We soon weep under the burden of personal responsibility which now falls upon us. Anxiety and guilt are inherent in that responsibility. The pressure from these drives generates the existential tension which permeates the intrapsychic dynamics of the self. The tension is rooted in the primary relationship of man with himself: I am alone in the room; there is no one here to force me into the pain of conflict; yet I have experienced moments of intense pain in just such a solitary state. There is something within my own being which forces me to examine and challenge myself. I reject psychological theories which reduce this demand upon myself to a mere by-product of my socialization. Rather the demand has an

---

[1]The dynamics of the existential encounter are described in Chapter 10: "The Metaphysics of Psychotherapy."

integrity and an energy source of its own. It manifests itself within me as an immediate reality, though its origin is obscured in the dense history of human evolution. It says something like this: "You are man; you are free; the alternatives before you are infinite; you alone must make a finite choice." It is the pain inherent in that choice which is being cut out of man by modern prophets. They offer him escapes. The right offers a new authority. The left offers the neutrality of "both/and" to eliminate the pain of "either/or." Still my condition remains critical. I do not respond to the "cure." I cannot escape the pain of crucial choice. I find no remedy for the "sickness" inherent in personal responsibility. I find no "cure" for the anxiety of freedom. It could be just an idiosyncratic ailment which afflicts only me. Yet I am convinced that no man can be free from the pain of choice and still be free to choose. The pain of conflict is inherent in the freedom of choice. It is a law of metaphysics as valid as those laws which govern events in the physical world. It is true that my vision of man could be twisted and malign. Still I cannot see man without freedom and I cannot see freedom without the painful anxiety of choice.

Nor can any social or political order imposed upon man alleviate the anxiety of existential choice. Any change in a society that is not a function of changes in the individuals who compose that society is only another form of tyranny. A "benevolent" tyranny is even more destructive because it drugs man with an illusion of freedom. Enhanced social status, increased social mobility, and greater social power do not give man existential freedom. Freedom is not a sociological category to be embodied in a political system. Freedom is an existential category to be encountered by the single individual alone. Man can never be *made* free by political systems, but he can always *be* free in spite of them. He is always free to choose his own reaction to any political event, even if that event were to be his own execution. Metaphysics concerns itself with the dynamics of this individual freedom and not with the sociology of political events. There can never be a political substitute for individual metaphysics. Yet innovative rapprochements between these two forces are possible. The lives of Gandhi and King provide us cogent models. These men generated significant *political* change as a function of their *metaphysical* commitment to the single individual: "Each one of us is a man!" Any constructive change must emerge from and be directed toward such radical commitment to individual integrity. The time is critical since contemporary social changes are a far greater threat to the survival of individual man than technological change. The metaphysical potential which has developed within the human individual is the highest achievement of evolution. It is that distinct potential which must be preserved to direct the destiny of man.

Anxiety is inherent in this metaphysics of human development because man has not attained his ultimate consummation. He is enmeshed in the tangled process of evolution. He has not become God in spite of many such claims. He has not even become man. The anxiety inheres in that fact. There is an existential tension between man and potential man. The tension generates an intrapsychic anxiety which cannot be eliminated by any simple formula to "accept yourself." The "death of God" did not make us Gods. It did not give us license to be "anything." It confronted us with the challenge to be that "something" which is man. We cannot escape the anxiety inherent in that challenge.

The challenge to be man embodies the struggle to relate with other men. Pain and guilt are bred into that struggle. The "front-office" physician who prescribes drugs[1] for "back-ward" patients can argue that psychological pain is obsolete. So can that argument be given by the psychologist who sets up a program of reinforcement for those same patients. They want to cut out pain the way a skilled surgeon cuts out a malignancy. They would better understand the significance of psychic pain if they entered one of those back wards. They would better understand psychic pain if they made direct contact with it. Such personal contact with pain would reveal that medication and manipulation do not heal these open sores of intrapsychic estrangement. Any treatment based on personal and professional distance but perpetuates the deeper cause of pain. Symptoms may be changed but the hurt inside bleeds ever more profusely. Only the interpersonal balm of a human encounter can close the festering wound of alienation. These "professionals" would soon discover that more than a prescription or a program was needed to make such interpersonal communion possible. It demands the personal labor of self-sacrifice and self-discipline. A therapist can encounter pain within another only if he encounters pain within himself. He can make a vital response to pain within the client only if he remains alive to his own existential pain. Yet the pain must be contained. It must be integrated into the self-structure so that it is useful but not disruptive. There is no easy way to develop and maintain such an integration. The self must struggle with itself and that struggle generates another tension state within existential man.

It is true that few of us will be asked to enter these particular back wards and to risk ourselves in these particular encounters. Yet the world is filled with back wards and the principle of interpersonal compassion is binding on us all. No man can be free from pain while any other one man still suffers. It is a law of metaphysics which binds

---

[1]Drugs are recommended by the conservative Right, on the basis of a biological model of man, as well as by the radical Left, on the basis of a psychological model of man. Both represent attempts to "cut out" metaphysical pain with no awareness of its existential significance for man.

man as surely as the law of gravity binds physical bodies. Yet man must choose even his response to the laws of his own nature. Only his choice to respond to the metaphysics of guilt can solve the critical human problem of man's alienation from man. Thus the existential self in man recognizes the constructive significance of anxiety and guilt. Existential man chooses anxiety to experience freedom. He chooses guilt to experience communion with his fellow man.

The tension demands upon the existential self do not end here. Other tension states are concomitant with the primary pain of anxiety and guilt. These are tensions which arise from the demand for conceptual organization of the self. They emerge from the basic tension between lived experience and the conceptual organization of that experience. There is no possible resolution of this tension state because there is no way to eliminate the conceptual demand. Conceptual organization is necessary to give meaning to experience. The conceptual integration of experience provides us with footholds from which we step deeper into existence. Conceptual organization is the heuristic process by which man penetrates further into the mystery of the human condition. Yet the need for conceptual organization confronts us with an existential tension between levels of awareness. There are processes of decision-making in man's struggle to be free which demand an explicit awareness of the significant variables on which a particular decision is to be based. Gods are Gods without effort and acorns become oaks without choice. Yet man must make himself man through the mundane labor of decision-making. He must focus his attention on the alternatives available and define the referent for his choice in such a way that differentiation among the available alternatives is possible. He must then choose the one alternative that best satisfies the referent criterion. The efficacy of that choice will be a function of the level of his awareness. He will choose the alternative which best fits the referent criterion if he has an explicit awareness of all the significant factors involved in the decision. Thus explicit awareness is necessary for effective decision-making. The converse is true for the expressive phase of any chosen action. Explicit awareness destroys the spontaneous expression of the self. The familiar centipede cannot walk when he is explicitly aware of his many legs. Yet there is no simple solution to this dilemma since impulsive action without self-awareness has no existential significance. An action is mine only if I am present in it. Thus I am confronted with the demand of another tension state. I must organize myself so that even my spontaneous expressions contain an implicit awareness of the self. The implicit awareness of the self in the expressive phase must relate back to the explicit awareness of the self in the decision phase. Yet the expressive self must have only an implicit awareness of itself and of this relationship. The tension is in the demand on the spontaneous self to resist a tendency to return to the security of explicit formulations, on the one hand, and to resist a counter tendency to abandon self-awareness and retreat to impulsive action, on the other. The more practiced the spontaneous self becomes in meeting this demand, the more vital is its existence. One aspect of the demand is an ability to make rapid shifts between the explicit and the implicit modes. For example, in psychotherapy an unexpected reaction by the client may force the therapist to make a sudden shift from an open mode of implicit expression to a closed mode of explicit formulation. It is only through the development of such capacities that man comes to know and value the significance of the existential self.

There is a bridge between the intrapsychic world of existential man and his interpersonal world. The bridge relates the solitary self to a world of other selves. It is not a simple bridge to cross. It, too, has its complex tensions. The stress in man's struggle to relate to his fellow man is in the effort to reconcile the solitude of the private self with an intersubjective communication of that same self. I must speak with others and at the same time remain silent. The silence dwells in the private self that is mine alone. I may say the same thing to another that I say to myself, but it has a different significance in these two dialogues. For example, I may tell a friend quite honestly about an event in my history. The mood between us will be a very personal one. Yet he knows the event has a different meaning to me alone than it does to us together. So does he appreciate the fact that I offer to him the same privacy even in our most personal moments. It is not that I want to exclude the other. Rather the recognition and constructive use of such privacy is the core of the existential self. My freedom and my love are both anchored in that privacy. It is the capacity to stand alone that makes me free. It is the capacity to stand alone that enables me to enter an interpersonal communion as an end in itself rather than as a means to gain support for an interdependent sociological self.[1]

This tension between the private and the personal self parallels the tension between the explicit and the implicit. We must function at the private and explicit level of awareness under social and psychological opposition. We shift to the personal and implicit level of awareness in interaction with those persons who are closer to us. We can enter into a process of open communication that is personal and implicit when we share a common ground and a common trust. Only a vague awareness of the private and explicit selves lingers in these relationships so that personal identities can be maintained. It is

---

[1]The client must speak aloud in psychotherapy, but only to discover the inward silence of the private self. It is only at the depths of such inward silence that man relates himself to existential truth. These dynamics are described in Chapter 10: "The Metaphysics of Psychotherapy."

during these personal and implicit moments that existential man gets a brief glimpse into the spiritual epoch of human evolution. The explicit/implicit and private/personal tension states are intrinsic to man's struggle for self-development and self-expression. The more effectively we can move within and between these modes of being, the more vital is our existence. These levels of awareness are complementary in spite of the inherent tensions between them. It is these tension states that existential man must confront and master.

Thus the death of God forces us into an encounter with the pain of our own existence. We must encounter the existential tensions in the intrapsychic self where man relates himself to himself and to the metaphysics of the human condition. So must we encounter the existential tensions of the interpersonal self where man relates himself to his fellow man. There are no escapes from the demands of existence at this critical stage of social change. We cannot build a separate culture and call it Heaven. Existential man must plant himself at the crossroads of human evolution prepared for the pain and labor of anxiety and guilt. Still do not pity me or other men who choose a similar stance—it is better to exist than to be happy.

The pages ahead contain specific examples of attempts to engage the client in such a critical struggle with his own existence. I do not promise him any drugs, any games, any short-cuts to a psychological Heaven. Rather I ask each client to "walk through the valley of the shadow of death" and promise only that he "will see through a glass darkly." Such is the fate of the existential self in each of us.

The Existential Ground
on existential rebellion

Kierkegaard: Concluding Unscientific Postscript

So there I sat and smoked my cigar until I lapsed into thought. Among other thoughts I remember these: "You are going on," I said to myself, "to become an old man, without being anything, and without really undertaking to do anything. On the other hand, wherever you look about you, in literature and in life, you see the celebrated names and figures, the precious and much heralded men who are coming into prominence and are much talked about, the many benefactors of the age who know how to benefit mankind by making life easier and easier, some by railways, others by omnibuses and steamboats, others by the telegraph, others by easily apprehended compendiums and short recitals of everything worth knowing, and finally the true benefactors of the age who make spiritual existence in virtue of thought easier and easier, yet more and more significant. And what are you doing?" Here my soliloquy was interrupted, for my cigar was smoked out and a new one had to be lit. So I smoked again, and then suddenly this thought flashed through my mind: "you must do something, but inasmuch as with your limited capacities it will be impossible to make anything easier than it has become, you must, with the same humanitarian enthusiasm as the others, undertake to make something harder." This notion pleased me immensely, and at the same time it flattered me to think that I, like the rest of them, would be loved and esteemed by the whole community. For when all combine in every way to make everything easier, there remains only one possible danger, namely, that the ease becomes so great that it becomes altogether too great; then there is only one want left, though it is not yet a felt want, when people will want difficulty. Out of love for mankind and out of despair at my embarrassing situation, seeing that I had accomplished nothing and was unable to make anything easier than it had already been made, and moved by a genuine interest in those who make everything easy, I conceived it as my task to create difficulties everywhere.

on metaphysical motivation

Berdyaev: Slavery and Freedom

Man, the only man known to biology and sociology, man as a natural being and a social being, is the offspring of the world and of the processes which take place in the world. But personality, man as a person, is not a child of the world, he is of another origin. And this it is that makes man a riddle. Personality is a breakthrough, a breaking in upon this world; it is the introduction of something new. Personality is not nature, it does not belong to the objective hierarchy of nature, as a subordinate part of it. . . . Personality cannot be recognized as an object, as one of the objects in a line with other objects in the world, like a part of the world. That is the way in which the anthropological sciences, biology, psychology, or sociology would regard man. In that way man is looked at partially: but there is in that case no mystery of man, as personality, as an existential centre of the world. Personality is recognized only as a subject, in infinite subjectivity, in which is hidden the secret of existence.

on intrapsychic dynamics (private self)[1]

Kierkegaard: Concluding Unscientific Postscript

Every human being is gloriously constituted, but what ruins so many is, among other things, also the wretched tittle-tattle between man and man about that which should be suffered and matured in silence, this confession before men instead of before God, this hearty communication between this man and that about what ought to be secret and exist only before God in secrecy, this impatient craving for intermediary consolation. No, in suffering the pain of his annihilation, the religious individual has learned that human indulgence profits nothing, and therefore refuses to listen to anything from that side; but he exists before God and exhausts the suffering of being human and at the same time existing before God. Therefore it cannot comfort him to know what the human crowd knows, man with man, what men know who have a shopkeeper's notion of what it means to be a man, and facile gossipy notion at seventeenth hand of what it means to exist before God.

---

[1]The private self exists before existential truth, which some call "God."

on interpersonal dynamics (personal self)

Kierkegaard: Concluding Unscientific Postscript

A double reflection is implicit in the very idea of communication. Communication assumes that the subject who exists in the isolation of his inwardness, and who desires through this inwardness to express the life of eternity, where sociality and fellowship is unthinkable, because the existential category of movement, and with it also all essential communication, is here unthinkable, since everyone must be assumed essentially to possess all, nevertheless wishes to impart himself; and hence desires at one and the same time to have his thinking in the inwardness of his subjective existence, and yet also to put himself into communication with others. This contradiction cannot possibly (except for thoughtlessness, for which indeed all things are possible) find expression in a direct form. That a subject who exists in this manner might wish to impart himself is not so difficult to understand. A lover, for example, whose inwardness is his love, may very well wish to communicate; but he will not wish to communicate himself directly, precisely because the inwardness of his love is for him essential. Essentially occupied constantly in acquiring and reacquiring the inwardness of love, he has no result, and is never finished. But he may nevertheless wish to communicate, although he can never use a direct form, because such a form presupposes results and finality. . . . Direct communication presupposes certainty; but certainty is impossible for anyone in process of becoming, and the semblance of certainty constitutes for such an individual a deception. Thus, to make use of an erotic relationship, if a loving maiden were to long for the wedding day on account of the assured certainty that it would give her; if she desired to install herself as wife in a legal security, exchanging maidenly longing for wifely yawning, her lover would have the right to complain of her unfaithfulness, and that although she loved no one else; because she had lost the Idea constitutive of the inwardness of love, and did not really love him. And it is this which characterizes all essential faithlessness in the erotic relationship; loving another is accidental.

on existential Hell (labor)

Camus: The Myth of Sisyphus

The gods had condemned Sisyphus to ceaselessly rolling a rock to the top of a mountain, whence the stone would fall back of its own weight. They had thought with some reason that there is no more dreadful punishment than futile and hopeless labor. . . . Sisyphus is the absurd hero. He *is,* as much through his passions as through his torture. His scorn of the gods, his hatred of death, and his passion for life won him that unspeakable penalty in which the whole being is exerted toward accomplishing nothing . . . one sees merely the whole effort of a body straining to raise the huge stone, to roll it and push it up a slope a hundred times over; one sees the face screwed up, the cheek tight against the stone, the shoulder bracing the clay-covered mass, the foot wedging it, the fresh start with arms outstretched, the wholly human security of two earth-clotted hands. At the very end of his long effort measured by skyless space and time without depth, the purpose is achieved. Then Sisyphus watches the stone rush down in a few moments toward that lower world whence he will have to push it up again toward the summit. He goes back down to the plain.

It is during that return, that pause, that Sisyphus interests me. A face that toils so close to stones is already stone itself! I see that man going down with a heavy yet measured step toward the torment of which he will never know the end. That hour like a breathing-space which returns as surely as his suffering, that is the hour of consciousness. At each of those moments when he leaves the heights and gradually sinks toward the lair of the gods, he is superior to his fate. He is stronger than his rock . . . his fate belongs to him. His rock is his thing . . . he knows himself to be the master of his days. . . . I leave Sisyphus at the foot of the mountain. One always finds one's burden again. But Sisyphus teaches the higher fidelity that negates the gods and raises rocks. . . . The struggle itself toward the heights is enough to fill a man's heart.

on existential Hell (pain)

Kierkegaard: Concluding Unscientific Postscript

The clergyman says indeed that the life of the cloister was an evasion of the danger, and that it is a greater thing to remain among the perils of life. . . . Let us at any rate try to understand one another, and seek to agree as to what we mean by the danger. The candidate for the cloister saw his greatest danger in the failure to sustain each moment an absolute relationship to the absolute telos . . . the absolute danger . . . the absolute exertion . . . the intercourse with the absolute in the stillness of solitude where the least loss is an absolute loss and the least retreat is utter ruin; where the mind is not diverted by distractions, but the memory of ever so slight an infidelity is a fire that burns and from which there is no escape, paralyzing the individual like a sunstroke; where every weakness, every faint moment, every disinclination, is as if it were a mortal sin, and every such hour is like an eternity, because time will not pass . . . and this life is what the clergyman calls an evasion of the danger. But he praises the courage of those who remain in the relative dangers, the dangers of the manifold, where the simplest experience teaches us that one never loses everything . . . that a loss in one place is made up for by a gain in another.

Part II

Encounters

Chapter 3
The Congruent Encounter

I want to understand more deeply the process of psychotherapy. I want to understand more deeply how man heals man. I want to thrust myself down into its obscure depths.

I heard a life born in the passion of the therapeutic process. I heard the life of one man make possible the birth of another. I want to understand the decisive movement which gives life force to such interpersonal encounter.[1]

I push down into my own experience and try to hold the movement closer to me. It is the one movement which makes psychotherapy a vital process for me. The therapeutic imperative is my congruent dedication to the reality of my own subjective experience. I comprehend the subjective reality of another only in my own deep commitment to the subjective reality which is me. I make a relationship real to another only by my own real participation in that relationship. I demand from myself a disciplined congruent participation in the subjective encounter between myself and the client. I want to explore that crucial movement more closely.[2]

I told a seductive but frigid female client, "I want to attack you sexually; I want you to explode and overflow." It was a mixed literal and figurative communication. The literal component of the movement was real and it was mine. Yet it was encompassed in the deeper figurative reality of a desire for personal therapeutic involvement. My own congruent participation forged the abstract relationship between us into a concrete experiential "now." Such an interpersonal "now" could not be cast from a direct communication of the figurative desire for an open therapeutic relationship. Therapeutic encounter

---

[1] I refer to a recorded interview by Dr. Carl Rogers with a young "schizophrenic" man. The life force of the interview was in the deep subjective participation of Dr. Rogers in the relationship. The healing encounter was fostered by: "I don't know whether this will help or not, but I would just like to say that . . I think I can understand pretty well . . what it's like to feel that you're *no damn good* to anybody, because there was a time when . . I felt that way about *myself* . . and I know it can be *really rough*"; and the dramatic change precipitated by: "Uh huh . . uh huh . . that's why you want to go . . because you really don't care about yourself . . you just don't care what happens . . and I guess I'd just like to say . . *I* care about you . . and *I* care what happens."

[2] *Congruent* is used here as developed in the context of Client-centered therapy.

is made from sterner stuff. She could have tactfully avoided an encounter with an abstract figurative me. Yet she did respond to the concrete me deeply involved in the personal moment between us. She could grasp a literal concrete participation. She could hold on to it and to me. Our literal involvement in the possibility of an open sexual experience moved us into the intended figurative reality of an open experiential relationship.

In a similar way the concrete participation of a client in the literal "I felt so bad I wanted to shoot myself" moves him deeper into the figurative reality of depression. The literal "I felt so mad I wanted to kill him" moves him deeper into the figurative reality of aggression. These are common literal-figurative communications by clients which are familiar to all of us. These literal concrete steps seem footholds toward deeper immersion in the intended experiential phenomena themselves. Just as literal rape was not intended here, neither is literal suicide or murder intended in most cases. These literal participations rather serve to move one deeper into the respective experience of intimacy, depression, or aggression.

These expressive modes point to experiential phenomena in a manner related to metaphorical participation. Yet literal-figurative participation involves one more directly in the intended experience itself. A metaphor points to an experience from a phenomenon which is distinct from the experience but parallel to it. The phenomenon of a tornado is distinct from an experience of rage though it is parallel to it. Participation in the metaphor "tornado" does not become an experience of rage as readily as does participation in the literal "I felt like beating and kicking him." The more direct personal involvement in literal-figurative participation follows from the more direct relationship between the literal and the figurative. The metaphor is a phenomenon which parallels the intended experience. The literal is a *concrete expression* of that experience. The literal and the figurative are but two expressive forms of the same experiential phenomenon. Consequently, involvement in the concrete literal form involves one almost as directly in the base figurative form itself. An involvement by client and therapist in the literal form, "I want to attack you sexually; I want you to explode and overflow," involves them almost as directly in the intended figurative form of an open experiential relationship.

Further examples of my own congruent participation in other relationships are: "I feel sad when you withdraw like that" and "you do seem a little crazy to me right now." These direct participations were encompassed and communicated in the deeper subjective tone of "let us be experientially open to each other." The direct involvement of the therapist in a personal movement toward the client transformed the figurative "I would like to be with you" into a concrete literal, "I am here now." The client cannot find himself in relation to my figurative participation. There is no real other there for him to feel and to encounter. Yet he *can* discover himself as he explores his relation to my concrete participation. He *can* feel his own reality in his subjective encounter with the reality of me. I am not distant and ambiguous as in analytic or non-directive methods. Rather I am there as a *concrete* person immersed in the *concrete* moment between us. Such personal involvement is for me the generative force in the process of psychotherapy. I let the other know that I am there, that I am real, and that I am deeply committed to our common bond of therapeutic encounter.

Congruent participation seems to me the most appropriate description for such personal involvement by the therapist. No new conceptual term such as "disclosure" is needed since I propose only the functional use of congruence itself. I want only to experience the nucleus of the therapeutic process more directly in the therapeutic encounter between myself and the client. I am congruent in my empathy and congruent in my positive regard but *direct* congruent participation is for me the most exigent expression of congruence. A term such as "disclosure" seems an inaccurate description for the expression of congruence which concerns me here. It connotes some disclosure *about* the therapist rather than a direct experiential participation *of* the therapist in the personal encounter between himself and the client. Congruent participation seems a parsimonious and accurate description for the proposed functional use of congruence.

The contrast of congruent participation to directive and interpretive methods is more marked. The therapist in those methods communicates *something about the client* to the client. The therapist in congruent participation communicates *something of himself* to the client. It is not the directive, "*you* want to sleep with your father." It is rather a personal communication *from* the therapist of his own subjective feeling toward the client, "*I* want to attack you sexually; *I* want you to explode and overflow." Such literal-figurative communication is an attempt to construct an occasion for open experiential interaction between client and therapist. Directive and interpretive communications *about the client* inherently limit the spontaneous span of his subjective participation. These restrictions inherently limit the spontaneous vitality of client-therapist interaction itself. But a congruent participation *of the therapist* presents both to the client and to the relationship an *open* range of subjective possibility. I make an encounter vital for myself and for the client only by such a personal venture into it. I care for a relationship only when I give something of myself to it. I can ask of the client only what I myself am not afraid to do. It is true that the communicated mood of subjectivity may turn the client away from rather than closer toward deeper personal participation. Yet only by such a risk of myself and of the relationship can I ask a client to risk his own subjective self in the process of personal discovery. So is it true that a rash impulsive move by the therapist may overwhelm the client and possibly the therapist himself. It is only a "disciplined" congruent participation that can bring client and therapist into constructive interaction in the interpersonal process of psychotherapy.

The theoretical assumption underlying congruent participation is that we can know another only from deep within ourselves. I can know another only from my own knowledge of myself. I can be with another only to the depth that I can be there with myself. The more real I become in the relationship, the more real the other becomes to himself and to me. A further assumption is that when I reach toward another from within myself, something of that gesture will be heard and answered by the other. He will know I am there and he will respond to it.

Such concrete personal participation is difficult but necessary. Figurative participation provides no means by which to attain its own proposed end. It is not a tangible substance which can be molded into the intended subjective encounter. But literal participation is in itself a workable means-end combination. It is solid material which the client can weld into an authentic encounter. In another example, a client avoided the figurative me but she did respond to the literal, "If you walk out now I will not be, as you put it, professionally 'miffed' —I will be personally hurt by your pulling away from me." She felt my presence and she responded to it.

I want to distinguish literal-figurative participation from other forms of communication. It is distinct from the double-bind as a therapeutic technique since the messages are not contradictory but are two forms of the one same message. So is it distinct from removed partial participations such as, "I had a thought, a dream, a fantasy, etc." These shared fantasies may even vitiate potentials for authentic interpersonal encounter. The participation I propose is the communication of one's deepest subjective *reality*. Nor is it a description by the therapist of his congruence. Rather it is a direct *expression* of that congruence in the experiential intimacy between himself and the client. Congruent participation is not a waiting to use congruence in an empathic response. It is a congruent movement into the relationship to develop an encounter *for* empathic communication. It involves the therapist in a rhythmic process of reaching toward and responding to the emotional existence of the client. Such a use of congruence can transform an abstract distant relationship into a concrete personal encounter. Congruent participation thus makes congruence an independent functional process as well as a necessary adjunct to the related processes of empathy and positive regard.

I have tried to describe what I mean by congruent participation. I would now like to discuss necessary discipline. The discipline demanded here is the acceptance of the pain of one's own aloneness. I must participate in the life of another, yet live in the deeper reality that each of us is ultimately alone. I can do no more than experience my own autonomy to construct an occasion for the autonomous experience of the client. So must I live in the sometimes pain of my solitude to make his autonomous experience possible.

In the congruence of my own solitude I cannot participate in the description a young female client gives of her extramarital involvements. She describes them as "innocent and platonic," yet they disrupt the marriages of those men with whom she is involved and now threaten her own fourth marriage. I reach from deep down within my subjective self toward the subjective depth of the client, "I do not understand . . how innocent and platonic relationships . . do such damage." The risked venture fails; she rejects my participation as an inappropriate reaction. It does not resonate in her own subjective awareness. She reasserts the validity of her own initial attitude. We are at a therapeutic impasse. One disciplinary mode of aloneness must now converge on and be transformed into a related mode. One mode demands that my participation be given to the relationship congruently bound as my own so that it does not impose itself on the experiential world of the client. It apparently was a disciplined participation since she recognized it as mine and felt free to assert the autonomy of her own attitude against it. I must now live the deepest part of my congruence in the pain of my own solitude. I must suffer the hurt that I cannot now be my deepest congruent self with her. I must retreat silently into the pain of my own aloneness. I must transform my congruence into a modified form of congruent participation. I must temporarily suspend part of myself to make myself free to congruently participate with her in experiential attitudes which are not me. Such *modified* congruent participation is the most that can be done. There is no other way to participate congruently in an experience which contradicts my own personal congruence. I must suffer the distance between us in the hope that a common experiential reality may emerge to which I can give my deepest congruent self. I must remain dedicated to my own congruence even when modified congruent participation is necessary. Only the therapist who does remain dedicated to his own congruence has a deepest congruent self to give should a common experiential reality emerge between himself and the client.

I find these modes of discipline very difficult to maintain, but they do seem to provide necessary guidelines for subjective participation. They do seem to give the proposed movement an effective posture. Even a rejected participation which is thus disciplined may move the interaction between therapist and client closer toward the intended personal encounter. Even a failure was still a direct expression of therapist congruence followed by a direct expression of active concern for the client's divergent attitude. Congruent participation and *modified* congruent participation both seem to be constructive interpersonal gestures even under the *least* favorable conditions.

Congruent participation is for me an experientially appropriate process since it explicitly demands from the therapist the personal venture which he implicitly demands from the client. Only the dedicated personal involvement of client and therapist in a common experiential reality is therapeutic. We are both there; we are both real; we know each other. The common experiential base is not used to provide client and therapist with reciprocal support. Such a use of mutual participation defeats its own end to develop the personal autonomy of each particular individual. The common base is used rather to provide a core reality to which we can both give our own deepest selves. It is only in such a dedicated venture of our selves that we discover our selves and our relationship to each other. I have found congruent participation helpful to me and to my clients. It transforms a passive client-centered approach into a more active and more versatile psychotherapy. It transforms psychotherapy itself into a method of existential encounter. Consequently, I describe the emergent process as "Encounter Therapy."

Chapter 4
The Modified Encounter

I want to enter the world of the other. I want to experience a communion with him. I struggle for a way. Empathy is a way:

> C. And then in another sense, I thought, well . . maybe it's just something I *have* to go through alone . .
>
> T. Maybe it's just hopeless to wish that I could really be in a relationship with anybody . . maybe I *have* to be alone . .
>
> C. And it's really a frightening kind of loneliness because I don't know who could be with you . . and it seems rather . .
>
> T. Is this what you're saying? . . Could anyone be with you in . . in fear, or in a loneliness like that? . . (pause) . . (Client weeps) . . (pause) . . just really cuts so deep . . (pause) . .
>
> C. I don't know . . (pause) . . is it just something you just have to . . really be intensely alone in and . . well, I just felt that way this week . . dreadfully, dreadfully all by myself sort of thing . .
>
> T. Hmm . . just a feeling as though you're so terribly alone . . in the universe, almost, and whether . . whether anyone could help . . you don't know . .
>
> C. I guess, basically there'd be a part of it you would have to do alone . . I mean, you couldn't take anybody else along in some of the feelings . . and yet, it would be a comfort, I guess, not to be alone . .
>
> T. It surely would be nice if you could take someone with you a good deal of the way into your . . feelings of loneliness and fear . . (pause) . .
>
> C. I guess I just have . . (pause) . .
>
> T. Maybe that's what you're feeling right this minute . . (pause) . .

Such an encounter is cogent testimony to the therapeutic significance of empathy.[1]

---

[1] This interview by Dr. Rogers with *Miss Munn* (Tape 5) and the interview cited earlier by Dr. Rogers with *Mr. Vac* (Tape 3) are both available through the Tape Library of the American Academy of Psychotherapists, 6420 City Line Avenue, Philadelphia, Pa.

Empathy is a way to understand. The process of being understood
does heal. Yet such knowledge must be but a point of departure. The
task now is to discover modes of therapist involvement which can
construct an encounter when the reflective mode of empathy has
failed. I begin here.

A young male client argues: ". . you can understand, et cetera, et
cetera, et cetera, but where is there anything between us!" I had failed.
The reflective mode had not fused an experiential bond between us.
Yet I had pushed empathy to its limit through a wide range of fears:

Honosexuality

C. Well, I don't trust men particularly . . this is kind of
ridiculous, but I really got this thing going about queers,
'cause I've had so many run-ins with them . . and getting to know an older man, I'm always, you know, kind
of half worried about . . well, is this guy a homo and
putting the "make" on me, or what . . and you know,
in your case, I'm sure, you know, I don't think it's so
. . it's just something I got and . . I don't know . .
T. So when I said I wanted to make you a real person
in my life . . I really wanted to know you . . to
you it had sort of an overtone of maybe I'm really
trying to queer you, and that's about all there is to it . .
C. (Laughs) Yeah . . well, you know, and I can't help
it . . it's just a thing I get inside me, and it really bugs
me 'cause sometimes I think I got, you know, bad homosexual tendencies, and this bothers me too . .
T. You're not sure again whether this reaction is always
in the other or maybe in you . . where is the darn thing
is what worries the hell out of you sometimes, I guess . .
C. Yeah, 'cause I don't want anything to do with queers,
you know, any type of homosexual activity kind of makes
me sick . . you know, they can be like that and I'm
not going to bug 'em about it, but I don't want to be
in it . . and yet again, I can't . . sometimes I wonder,
you know . .
T. I guess you're saying you haven't really come to direct
terms with this whole issue of homosexuality . .
C. No, I haven't . . I can't figure it out, it's kind of,
for me it's frightening not to know if I'm, you know . .
what the deal is . .
T. Not to know when you're with a man whether he's
going to try to seduce you, or you're going to want him
to seduce you, or . .

C. Yeah . .

T. To know exactly what this sexual business between you and a man might be all about . .

Impotence

C. Yeah . . and then if I have sort of nasty things going with girls sometimes, which has happened, well then, Christ, I just, you know, I'm really bugged by it then . . and then I start thinking, Christ, maybe I don't dig girls at all, and it's embarrassing besides . .

T. Then if something goes bad with a woman, that's painful enough in and of itself, but it makes you think, by God, maybe these fears I have are real . .

C. It sure had me worried the first time it happened, and the second time it *really* bugged me (laughs) . . I don't even like to think about it . . if I do, you know, God, it's kind of frightening . .

T. It's sort of a blow to a guy (laughs) . .

C. It is, and then to have a girl ask you to make love to her and you can't do it, well, shit, you know, and after getting yourself sort of built up in her eyes as a big Don Juan, well . .

T. You can do everything but . .

C. Right, and then . . you know . . the excuses I come up with . .

T. (Intense laughter) . .

C. (On verge of intense laughter) . . Sometimes I come up with some of the most beautiful God damn excuses in my life . . you know, things that they believe completely but they were just so weird . . and I knew I was making an excuse, so I sort of saved myself in her eyes, but it didn't save myself in my eyes at all . .

Masturbation

C. I used to worry about masturbating too much, then I decided that was ridiculous . .

T. It's been a little easier to deal with masturbation than with the, oh, sometimes failure with women and the fear of homosexuality . . those three things all cause you some concern, I guess . .

C. Yeah . . you know the thing with masturbation is, you know, when you're a little kid you're always told a bunch of shit about it . . well, you know it was a bunch of crap and yet I couldn't help wondering, well, maybe

down, way the hell down deep inside, I am being bugged
by this thing, and I don't even realize it's bothering me
. . that's what gets so confusing . . the fact that I realize
that maybe things really are bothering me, but I'm not
aware of the fact that they're bothering me . .
T. That is, you think maybe way down inside there is
some truth to those "old wives' tales" about masturbation . .
C. Yeah . . you know 'cause it's bothering me and it
could affect me without my being aware of it . . that's
what's so difficult about knowing myself . . I never
know what's way down inside and how it's affecting
me . . I just got the surface and I can control it . .
T. You sound as if you're pretty sure that, way down
deep, there is quite a bit of fear about some of these
things . .
C. Yeah . . there must be judging from my actions . .

Inadequacy
C. I've always sort of had the feeling that I'm not
adequately equipped, so to speak, you know, but I
don't know if it bothers me or not . . I can act like it
doesn't, yet I suppose really it does . . you know, it
would be nice to be quite large, I suppose, but you know . .
T. Uh huh . . you think all these things about your
being inadequate and homosexual . . and now you
don't even have a big cock . .
C. (Laughs) Right . . (laughs) but I don't know how
much that worries me, you know, because, well, you
know, I could always use the excuse before anyway . .
it's not quantity but quality, but shit, now I can't even
make love . . (laughs) hells bells!
T. Before, the old adage that it's what you do with it,
not what you have, sounded good to you . . but now
even that (laughs) . .
C. (Laughs) Now I'm, you know . .
T. Yeah . .
C. Christ, I'm all fucked-up . . I don't know why this
thing should bother me . . what the hell difference does
it make how large it is or isn't . . except there's so
much emphasis in our society placed on this thing, you
know, especially when boys get together, you know,
all bragging and everything, and . .
T. The bigger the penis . .

C. Yeah . .

T. The more masculine the guy . .

C. Yeah, right . . and I'm not really what you'd call a masculine looking person anyway, you know, and all these things, you know, sort of ganging-up together seem to be creating problems maybe . .

T. Yeah . . you're getting a lot of pressure toward thinking you're just not a man at all, I guess . .

C. Yeah . . I guess so, but damn it, it just shouldn't bother me . .

Prejudice

T. You think maybe these might be some of the monsters you're afraid might really . .

C. Yeah . . they're something that I got . . like prejudice . . I'm not at all prejudiced as far as I know . . but maybe, way down deep inside again, I am . . and that would make me just sort of almost a hypocrite . . and that really bothers me . . just about everything that, you know, I feel strongly about . .

T. Almost everything you really value is potentially unreal to you . .

C. Yeah . .

T. 'Cause you think if you knew the *real* you about all this, by God, what a thing that might be . .

C. Yeah . . but I, you know I never can get in on it . .

T. I guess the real you might be a . .

C. (Laughs) Real . . mean . .

T. Prejudiced, masturbating, inadequate, homosexual . .

C. Homosexual, exactly (laughs) . . you got me . . you know it's not a very pleasant thought, I guess . . so I won't think about it . . the hell with thinking . .

None of these empathic attempts had been successful:

T. You know, all that we do when we keep bringing up these things is just sort of fill in more possible reasons why you might be insecure and unable to find a definite way for yourself in the world . . and yet all we do is compound the picture . . we don't seem to break through at any point . .

The reflective mode had failed. Empathy had not made "anything between us!" Yet I knew there *was* something between us. I struggled for a way to forge that something into a therapeutic encounter. I explored beyond empathy and found "congruent participation":[1]

> C. I was kind of wondering if one reason why it's harder for me to establish anything with you, and with most people probably, that aren't like me . . maybe that's why 'cause they're not kind of bums, screwed-up or wondering, or anything . . maybe I feel that I can't trust them 'cause it'd be so much easier for them to reject me . . cause it'd be so easy for them to say, "Here's this guy who's all screwed-up so I won't have anything to do with him" . . people that I go around with are all screwed-up themselves so they can't really say, "He's a bum; he's wasting his life; I don't want anything to do with him" . . but people who aren't like this, they can do that and I guess sometimes they do . . they don't want anything to do with me . . maybe I just don't work really all the way at establishing anything if I don't feel an immediate bond . . (pause) . .
>
> T. You don't . . you don't feel that . . that I know what it is . . to be fucked-up right . .
>
> C. Of course I know this . . but it's not a question of me sitting here saying to myself that I know that you know what it's like to be fucked-up and everything . . that has nothing to do with this . . what the hell . . so I know this . .
>
> T. You mean . . you don't feel that I as a person . .
>
> C. I feel it consciously . . but what about inside? . .
>
> T. You don't feel the fucked-up me inside yourself! . .
>
> C. No . . you're . . you know . . like with "Duke," he's all screwed-up; immediately I felt sort of a something between us . . you know, with most people I don't 'cause they're not like that . . and oh, consciously I can say to myself that, you know, you can understand, et cetera, et cetera, et cetera . . but where is there anything between us! . .
>
> T. I have to look at you as something different from me to understand . .
>
> C. Maybe that's it . .
>
> T. I can't feel with you the way he does . . (pause) . .

---

[1]The interaction which follows is taken from a sequence of recorded excerpts published by the Tape Library of the American Academy of Psychotherapists (Tape 2).

you don't . . you don't feel . . that part of me never really gets through to you . . all the unknown, ambiguous, dark corners in my life . . my past, my present, and possibly the future . . you don't sense those . .

C. No, as a matter of fact, I never have at all . . like with "Duke," we can talk about things . . like yesterday we sat down on the beach for awhile and we were both very tired because we didn't go to bed 'til about 6:30 in the morning yesterday either . . and we just sort of looked at each other and said, "How fucking ridiculous . . we're wasting our lives doing absolutely nothing and all we can do is laugh about it" . . and finally I said, "Shit, this is ridiculous, we're all fucked-up and we know it, we don't even care enough to do anything more than laugh" . . we sat there and (laughs) "wow, wow, we're all fucked-up, look what we're doing" (laughs) . .

T. You really get a kick out of that shared realization of just craziness . .

C. Then we just sat there and laughed at ourselves . . we don't even care enough . . we care so God damn little that we just sit here and laugh because we're all fucked-up . .

T. I guess you both, really most of you at that moment just doesn't give a damn about the fact that your lives are nothin' . .

C. I know, I said I don't even care right now . .

T. Yeah . .

C. I'm laying in the warm sand and the warm sun, laughing (laughs) . . laughing at me (laughs) . .

T. And each laugh sort of sinks you deeper into the sand 'til finally you probably won't even be able to breathe, but you don't really care, you're still laughing . .

C. Right (laughs) . .

T. Well, I guess my problems aren't laughable to me the way they are to you and your buddy, so I can't . .

C. Well, they aren't laughable, this is what pissed me off yesterday 'cause I said, "What the shit am I laughing at them for!" . . but I had to admit that I right now, right then, just couldn't give a shit less . . so I'm all fucked-up, big deal. I'm going to sit here and laugh about it . . and so I'm laughing at it, how silly of me, and that's all we could do about it was just laugh . .

T. But you can find someone who will . . and the person I guess you feel closest to now is someone who

can really be with you in that 'cause that's his attitude
toward himself as well . . you can both share that
crazy mixed-up attitude . .

C. Yeah, because I guess my problems aren't serious
to me most of the time . . once in a while I get sort of
pissed off, overwhelmed with them, but the rest of the
time I just sort of shrug it off with this control thing I've
got . . no big thing, you know; I'll sit up here and talk
to you about it, but I won't worry even about the immediate problems . . I guess one time I did 'cause I was
worried I couldn't make love and I was worried about
being homosexual, then I was worried . . but the rest
of this shit, you know, I say my mother beat me, I hate
my mother; my father was just nothing so I don't like
my father, I suppose maybe I hate him more than my
mother, but I just say that, sounds good I guess, I don't
know, and I talk about it . .

T. Yeah . . you can't really get involved in those
things, I guess . .

C. No, I just say 'em . .

T. Hmm, hmm . .

C. They don't worry me anymore . . I mean I don't
let them worry me any more . . I'm not bothered by
them anymore, where it shows . . so my mother hated
me . .

T. Yeah . .

C. My father was an asshole, so what . .

T. It has nothing to do with you, I guess . .

C. Big deal! I had a bitchin' mother, and . .

T. But being queer and inadequate . . that has something to do with you right now . . it's harder to turn
that away than something that happened in the past . .

C. But I don't like to be bothered by it either, so I don't
bother with it very often . . I'm not queer, of course
not, why should I be . . so I can't make love (laughs)
. . what a joke . .

(Climactic laughter by both C. and T.)

C. Fuck, Jesus Christ, what a fucking joke, well no
man . .

T. You're an inadequate queer and so what . .

(More laughter)

C. That's not so funny really . .

T. I don't see why not . .

C. Well . .

T. What's wrong with . . I mean I really don't see, and I can get a little feeling of that, so what . . you're an inadequate queer, so what, I don't even care . .

C. (Laughs) That's horrible . . no, I should care . . (Climactic laughter again by both C. and T.)

T. Who told you that?"

C. No, shit, Jesus Christ, I like to . . I, you know, fuck . . I don't want to be a queer and I want to fuck . . but you know, if I can't, so what . .

T. (Intense laugh) . .

C. What a piece of shit that is . . if I can't feel something about that, for Christ's sake . . feel about fucking . . God, fucking's a weird word . . what a weird word . .

T. Fucking asshole strikes me as a weird word . . (laughs) . .

C. Yeah, but fucking . . what a sound, what a sound . . fuck . . how the hell did they ever invent fuck . . fuck you . .

T. (Laughs) It's a good word though . .

C. Really . . it's so feeling . .

T. We don't know which came first, the feeling or the word, but the word is . . mother-fuckin' is another good word . .

C. But when I think of the word fuck . .

T. Mother-fuckin' . . I like mother-fuckin' too . .

C. Yeah . .

T. You don't like mother fuckin'? . .

C. Yeah . .

T. You like mother fuckin'! . .

C. I don't use it very often, I don't think, but it's . .

T. I even like cock-sucker too . . but I don't think you do (laughs) . .

C. Yeah, I do . .

T. Mother-fuckin' cock-sucker is a good one . .

C. Yeah, it is . .

T. You like it . .

C. Yeah, it's got such a sound . . such a filthy rotten sound to it . . it's so dirty . . when I think about making love to a girl, I don't really think about fucking . . fucking is an insult . . fucking is dirty, filthy rotten, and mean, and evil and everything . . fucking is taboo . . fucking is filthy, it's a filthy sound . . fuck . .

> T. It even sounds, you know the actual process is juicy
> and it could be fuck, fuck . .
> C. Right . .
> T. Juice, juice kind of thing . .
> (Laughter once more by both C. and T.)

Now neither of us wondered any longer "where is there anything
between us?"

> C. I guess if I'm with somebody that . . that won't
> hold it against me . . and who goes through it him-
> self . . and understands, maybe not completely, but
> understands at least how I feel about it . . and under-
> stands that I do laugh at it . . somebody just as fucked
> up as I am . . then I can drop the smile and the big
> laugh . . even then we can laugh at it but, by God, I
> realize I'm laughing at it and I can say, "Why the fuck
> am I laughing at it?" . . but even then it sometimes
> becomes too much words, too much saying well maybe
> it's this, maybe it's that, maybe I did this, maybe this
> happened . . but still it's a little closer than it is with
> anybody else anytime . .

My active participation in his bizarre world had produced an
encounter where empathy failed.

I try to understand why something more than empathy was
needed. "People who aren't like me . . I can't trust them" seems the
answer. The failure to trust underlies all therapeutic failure. An
emotional climax is possible only in a relationship of trust. Only then
can energy otherwise needed for emotional defense be used instead
for emotional expression. Only such a concentration of expressive
energy can produce an emotional climax. Climactic laughter, tears,
etc. can then break through and overflow the relationship barrier
between client and therapist. Such an interpersonal climax is essential
to successful psychotherapy. It is the climactic experience of interpersonal trust. Empathy can often construct such a trust encounter.
It can often convince the client you are *enough* "like him" to be
trusted. Yet empathy sometimes fails. It had failed here. We did not
meet in my reflective responses to his phenomenal world. We met
instead when I entered his phenomenal world myself. At those
moments I *was* "like him" and he *did* trust me. My personal participation in his experiential world was the step beyond empathy which
generated a therapeutic encounter.

Such participation follows from a commitment to interpersonal pathos. A therapist must suffer the phenomenal experience of the client. No one can go beyond empathy in this generic sense. Rather varied modes to communicate felt pathos are needed. These modes can open therapy to new interpersonal possibilities. They are not substitutes for the reflective mode but adjuncts to a deeper expression of primal empathy.

We can experience interpersonal pathos because we choose our behavior from among alternatives. As we choose some alternatives, we abandon others. Yet we remain open to a much wider range of responses than those which we choose. We remain open to our *potential* self as well as to our chosen self. We can know the otherwise alien world of the client because of this extended range of experiential possibility. We can respond to him because his experience is within our own *potential* range. The task now is to discover varied modes which can express this capacity for interpersonal pathos. I have found the modes of "congruent participation" helpful for such expression.

I experienced a personal encounter by active entry into another bizarre experiential world. The interpersonal mood of the encounter was markedly distinct from the one already presented. The client I wanted to know was thirty-two years old and had been hospitalized for most of his adult life. He had lived the last five years, as he described it, "completely in the spirit world." He let me enter into that world with him during our third interview:

> (Long pause during which C. jerks his head and body almost convulsively, as if in contact with some unknown force)
> T. Are they here now? . .
> C. Yeah, they're here . .
> T. All three this time? . .
> C. No, just Jesus and Moses . .
> T. Jesus and Moses . . because Elijah was at home mostly . .
> C. Yeah . . (pause) . .
> T. I feel . . I feel . . (pause) . . Jesus . . but . . (pause) . . now I feel Moses a little too . . standing back farther . . and carrying something in his arms . . are those the commandments? . .
> C. Yeah . . (pause) . .
> T. Jesus . . Jesus seems to me to be crying for some reason . . I don't know why . . (pause) . . and he says he's worried . . about you . . that he knows you want to do right . . but he's worried . . (pause) . . it's not crying in the sense of sobbing but his eyes are moist . .

and once in a while a tear does gather at the corner of his eye . . and run down his cheek . . (pause) . . he seems to be holding his hand out to you . . don't you have any answer for him? . .

C. Not right off-hand . . (pause) . . (suddenly jerks his head and body again) . .

T. Did you get a sign then . . (pause) . . looks to me as if you're turning your back on him . .

C. On Jesus! . .

T. He's holding his hand out . . and you're not doing anything . .

C. I was talking to Moses . .

T. I see . . I'm sure Jesus will understand that . . but he seems . . he seems so . . so afraid and worried for you . . standing there with tears . . holding out his hand . . it even looks like both his hands now . . the robe draping over his arms . . and I thought you were standing sideways . . but you were talking to Moses and that was why . .

The dialogue in the spirit world continued until near the end of the hour. As we stood up to leave I reached over and touched him gently on the shoulder. He hesitated then put out his hand. I shook it quickly and he hurried down the hall. It is my hope that our encounter in his phenomenal world has produced an interpersonal awareness which will develop into a therapeutic relationship.

I experienced an encounter in still another distinct interpersonal mood with a female client troubled by her sexual promiscuity. She softened as she whispered, "I am afraid to experience myself fully here for fear I will seduce you." A reflective response seemed too constricted. I ventured a more personal participation. I entered into the seduction itself. We met in her experiential world. I suspended my deepest congruent self to participate in a modified congruence. I participated in the range of my potential rather than my chosen self. Those moments of personal participation developed a trust between us where empathy had failed. She knew now that I *was* "like her" and could be trusted. She knew now that I *did* understand her world but had made other choices for myself. The open relationship between us opened other life choices to her as well.

I have found these personal ventures into the distorted world of the client vital to the therapeutic process. They can often construct an authentic encounter when empathy has failed. I do not resonate with the phenomenal world of the client. I abandon that perspective to enter the phenomenal world myself. I abandon the asymmetrical mode of reflection to participate in a reciprocal interaction. I do not respond "as if I were the client." I respond as I experience my own potential self in interaction with him. I laughed as loud and swore as hard as the young male client. I moved as freely in the spirit world as did the hospitalized client. I experienced the seductive mood as intensely as the female client. I try to enter the intimacy of a *folie à deux* experience, yet control my own aberrant participation. The interpersonal phenomenon which results is for me as distinct and unique as the empathic phenomenon. I have found such participation an exploration beyond empathy into another valuable mode of interpersonal communion.

Chapter 5
The Body Encounter

A therapist once told me that he never touched the body of a client. He argued that "it distorted the nature of the therapeutic relationship." Such an aseptic approach intuitively disturbed me. Yet its authoritative finality also intimidated me. I am no longer so easily intimidated. I am now convinced that the therapist who will not touch a client with his body will not touch a client at all.

I want to understand body communication in psychotherapy. I must begin at the beginning. I must begin with my own personal experience. I must first note the reaction pattern of my own body.

I become aware of danger and experience fear. My body responds. It becomes tight and hard as a protective defense. I am in a trusted relationship and experience love. My body responds. It becomes warm and open to the other. My body responds to a deeper emotional me. A body language emerges from my deepest emotional self. A coherent and effective language emerges from an integrated emotional me. Body communication breaks down without such personal integration. Body language is only an expression of my deeper inward self. Its communication potential is determined by the degree to which that inward self is integrated and developed. Thus congruent body participation is but another mode by which the therapist can communicate his deepest subjective self to the client. It is but another mode for the expression of therapist congruence.

Such body expression is intimately related to deep emotional experience. Restrict body expression and you restrict emotional experience itself. Stop laughter and you abort an experience of joy. Stop tears and you abort an authentic encounter with despair. So too does a restriction of body participation in the process of psychotherapy abort authentic participation in that process. All modes of expression which facilitate deeper emotional experience must be an intrinsic part of psychotherapy. There can be no arbitrary restrictions on the modes of congruent participation. The very efficacy of these processes lies in their spontaneous emergence. They must be what they will.

A forty-two year old female client had a skin disease as a child. It concentrated primarily on the facial area. Her face had thus been the focus of much physical and emotional pain. It had even been the focus of frequent brutal assaults by a cruel guardian. Her complexion cleared as she matured. Yet the deeper wounds inside did not heal. She

37

seemed to experience the world as little more than a sequence of devastating facial attacks. She felt that I was a figurative part of this endless chain of insult and injury. She felt at one point that I too "slapped her face." Such crude failure to communicate my tender feeling for her much-abused person deeply hurt me. I answered haltingly, with tears in my eyes: "It hurts me so for you to feel I slapped your face . . when really . . I have felt how much . . I have wanted . . to touch your face . . gently . . and . . gently kiss your face." This expression of my implicit body involvement in the relationship dramatically transformed the mood between us. She had been suspicious and reserved. She became soft and intimate. It was in response to my implicit body gesture that she told me of her deeper self:

> C. Well, I may have been looking for that . . I may have interpreted it that way . . you see . . (pause) . . the woman who took care of me hated children . . just hated them with a horrible passion . . of course she had her hands full with me, there's no doubt about it . . I . . was ill . . for . . I shouldn't say I was ill . . (pause) . . (broken voice) . . I was disgusting to look at off and on for twelve years . . I had a hideous skin disease . . they had to shave off all my hair . . and my nose and ears and other parts of my face would crack and be hideous messes of sores . . this woman happened to like pretty things . . well, I like pretty things . . I don't think that's anything wrong . . like one time she said why couldn't I have been somebody on television or in show business or something . . why couldn't I have just been something pretty or talented . . well, I don't know why that wasn't worked out . . but she did have her hands full with me . .
>
> T. You seem to be saying . . you were so . .
>
> C. I was pretty ugly . . let's face it . . (strained laughter) . .
>
> T. You were so . . ugly . . at the time that you deserved to have your face slapped and beaten around . .
>
> C. (Hesitant) No . . no . . I don't think I deserved that, but with her being the way she was I guess she couldn't help it . . as I get older, I see these things . . when I was a child . . I can't remember too much outside of fear . . I definitely was afraid of her . . scared to death of her . . but I think I always believed that what she said was right . . in those days there was that

age-old question . . I remember it in the newspapers
. . heredity or environment . . which is the prime
factor of life? . . well, according to her, heredity was all
that counted . . she loathed my mother so, therefore,
I'm no good either . .

T. You had bad blood . .

C. Yeah . . I was just naturally born bad . . well, a
child doesn't know whether they're born bad or not so
who are they going to believe other than the person who
tells them the truth of the story . . if it is the truth . .
and I grew up thinking that this must be true . . that it
had to be true . . I couldn't question it as a child . . it
just had to be . . (pause) . . I put it out of my mind for
a long time until my own baby was born and then, little
by little, these things creep back into your mind . . but
as a child I couldn't question her . . I didn't have the
right to question her . . of course, I questioned her in
my eyes . . I'm sure I did that to her . . my little girl
does that to me . .

T. But deep down you believed you were an ugly
doomed child . .

C. Well . . I don't know that I believed I was doomed
. . I was a willful kid . . I decided someday I'd prove
her wrong . . I didn't know how but I knew I would . .

T. You were too willful to be beaten down, even by
her . .

She told me that she cried often when alone, but never in the
presence of another person. She had learned as a child to kill her
tears:

C. When I saw the guardian years later, she pointed out
to me that I was such a cold child . . and what she
pointed out was one of the things I hated her for . .
(pause) . . as I said, this disease was pretty hideous
and they used a medicine they said would burn like hot
coals . . and I can remember the pain . . when you
have it for years on end, and you get this stuff put on you,
and it's like someone . . it just is like hot coals put on
something . . if I cried she would beat me . . so I
wouldn't cry . . I would take the lesser of the two . .
fight the pain of the medicine rather than a beating . .
so I wouldn't cry . . and I wouldn't . . I just wouldn't
cry . .

T. You bit down hard and . .

C. (Emphatic) Oh . . I can remember it . . I don't guess you'll ever forget anything like that . . and this is what she told me last time I saw her . . that I was such a mean child I wouldn't cry even when she put that medicine on me . . and yet I know that why I didn't cry was if I cried I got a beating . .

T. That was the part she didn't mention . .

C. Yeah . . so I just looked at her . . and let the years go by . .

T. And when you might have cried . . she would threaten you with a beating and shock you out of it . . (pause) . . you really felt I had done this too . .

C. I don't know . . you know I may have because I was almost on a tear-jerker the other day . . something was said that I could have cried . . I don't know what it was . . and, if I look at my life sensibly, I don't think there's a thing in my life to cry about . . yet I do cry . . like something good happens on television and I want to bawl . . I don't think this is quite normal but . . the other night I could have cried when I was sitting there with my husband . . he said, "Why are you so sad?" . . and I couldn't tell him why I was so sad . . I don't know . .

T. And you can't tell me either, I guess . .

C. (Hesitant) No . . but I have felt if I could go on a good crying jag . . for say three days or something . . (strained laughter) . . maybe I would snap out of whatever I think is wrong with me . .

T. You usually recover from pain by choking off your tears . . now maybe you feel that you might come out different if you cried a good long time . . (pause) . .

C. Well . . one day I was angry and everything . . I cried . . I cried wildly . . it didn't help me . . so tears really don't help . . at least, maybe they do for a physical outlet . . a nervous outlet . . but mentally, tears aren't going to help me . .

T. You're pretty sure of that I guess . .

C. Well . . see, there again . . logic says to me, how can tears help mental disorder? . .

T. You can't find a logical why for that . .

C. No . . (pause) . .

T. I guess you feel that I must be opposed to your crying too . .

C. No . . I think you'd be very kind about it . . but I can't see that would serve your purpose or mine for me to sit here and cry . .

T. Not even if you really felt like crying . .

C. Well . . (strained laughter) . . the only thing I can say to that is, if I started crying, you might see a true picture of me in a light that I can't see . .

She continued to struggle with the possibility of tears. The next interview she described a deep need to feel emotionally close to someone. She talked intimately of crying with me. Yet she felt she could not cry unless I held her close in my arms. I answered that in my deepest self I felt I was holding her close to me. She seemed to need more now than an implicit body gesture. She knew I felt emotionally warm toward her. She seemed to need more. She seemed to need the security of my arms about her. She described how close she held her little girl when the child cried. She needed that same physical protection for her own tears. It was as if her abused body needed a more tangible proof of my commitment to our relationship. She needed the possibility of full organic participation to express her deepest emotional self.

A number of sessions intervened until the issue of physical involvement emerged again. She described wanting to walk with me and hold my hand close in her own. She told me how often she had thought of walking with me in such an intimate way. She seemed to be asking once more for a physical expression of our warm feeling for each other. She seemed to need it somewhere deep inside her. She needed to know that one person in the world did not want to abuse her or her body. At the end of the interview we walked slowly toward the door in deep interpersonal silence. As she turned to leave she looked softly into my eyes. Once more I felt as if I were holding her close to me. Yet, in that moment, it did not seem enough for either of us. It seemed abortive and dishonest to feel constructive body warmth, but not express it. I lifted her gently into my arms and held her close. She relaxed her whole being and pulled me to her. She whispered in an almost inaudible murmur: "Thank you." These few moments between us seemed to provide the body security she so needed. They were the bridge to an even deeper body involvement in the therapeutic process.

The next interview was five days later. It was our twelfth hour together. The client told me that she had been "on a five-day crying jag." Tears were not streaming down her cheeks but they filled the full space of her eyes. Only a bitter determination not to cry could have checked their flow. She looked directly at me and repeated with defiance: "I refuse to cry . . I refuse to cry." I pulled my chair up close to hers, took her hand gently in mine, and lifted her slowly and tenderly onto my lap. She nestled into my arms, her whole being relaxed once more, and then she sobbed and sobbed and sobbed. After an unknown time lost in tears and silence, she lifted herself back onto her own chair. We spoke softly, quietly, tenderly for the remainder of the hour. As the interview ended, this intimate body involvement seemed as natural to the therapeutic process as a tender spoken word or an empathic facial gesture. The body involvement was expressed in such a context of solemn communication that it no longer seemed a bold therapeutic venture. It seemed rather a natural interpersonal mode intrinsic to the organic flow of the process of psychotherapy.

So have I found congruent body participation effective with severely disorganized clients. It can often construct an encounter when other modes are of limited value. One such body encounter emerged during the twenty-second interview with a thirty-year old female client. She came to the session with lipstick painted on her face, as if prepared for some type of tribal rite. She paced around the room for the first part of the hour making bizarre sounds and gestures. Finally she sat down on the floor near my chair. She crawled over to me on her knees and looked up into my face. It was the only personal gesture amidst all the chaos and I wanted her to feel my presence during that critical moment. I put my right hand firmly on the back of her neck. She became frightened: "You want to kill me!" I continued to hold her firmly. She made a sudden move to pull away, then, as suddenly, buried her face in my lap. I held the back of her head and neck with both my hands. She overflowed with heavy and labored tears: "All that blood and pus is just pourin' out of me; that must be what's meant by healin'." She had been loud and vulgar but now she was quiet and soft. I dried her tears and wiped away what I could of the smeared lipstick. We walked back to the ward in gentle silence. Body participation had forged an intimate therapeutic encounter when other less personal modes had failed.

Nor is body communication in therapy limited to male-female relationships. A male client in a moment of crisis found that our clasping arms like two comrades was the turning point in his acceptance of his own masculine identity. Still a myth prevails that such body contact inevitably "distorts the nature of the therapeutic relationship." I have found it otherwise. I have expressed my body in a wide variety of relationships with a wide range of emotionally troubled persons. I have found in relationships open to all possible modes of interaction that those modes emerge which most facilitate the experience of psychotherapy. I may doubt all else, but I trust these deeper subjective processes in myself and in man.

Chapter 6
The Metaphor Encounter

The metaphor is a diffuse symbol. It connotes attributes of a concept beyond the denotative definition of that concept. Its efficacy is in that very diffuseness. It can penetrate more deeply the dense complexity of subjective experience. Schematized denotative symbols categorize and distort a phenomenon rather than penetrate its true complexity. The denotative definition of the concept *sailor* is "one who takes part in the practical management of a vessel." This definition places the concept in a category of class function, but nothing more. Such a definition ignores the subjective density of the concept. The metaphor *driftwood* for the concept *sailor* penetrates into that subjective density. It is an implicit statement that a sailor is like driftwood. As such it connotes emotional, motoric, and textural attributes of a sailor which are not expressed by the denotative definition. A sailor is described as emotionally aimless and unpredictable, motorically buoyed about by the sea, and texturally with a complexion worn by constant exposure to wind, water, and sun. The metaphor thus expresses subjective attributes of a phenomenon which cannot be expressed by the denotative symbol itself. Its efficacy is in such connotative vitality.

I value the metaphor because it cogently clarifies the object it represents. The metaphor is a cognitive symbol which makes consciously explicit the subjective nuances of a phenomenon. Emotional reactions are not directly evoked by metaphors, but rather they are indirectly induced by the cognitive clarity the metaphor gives to its object referent. The metaphor *driftwood* induces an emotional sense of futility and dissipation only because it makes consciously explicit certain cognitive attributes of the referent *sailor*. The metaphor is used in psychotherapy to clarify and communicate these nuances of subjective experience.

A young female client had just recovered from a critical phase of severe disorganization. She needed an expressive mode to clarify and communicate her struggle to become an integrated person. She found such a mode in her discovery of the metaphor. This was the path to that discovery:

> C. Like part of me is still gone and I have to find that
> part . . and I think I can get a hold of it except I don't

want to lose control over myself again . . I don't want
to get too emotional . .

T. You feel that in trying to get back your other self you
might get overwhelmed by emotion again . . that
coming back together might be too much for you to
control . .

C. Let's see if I can say it . . like this other self would be
good for me, if I knew how to handle it . . if I didn't
let it overtake this part of me . . if I could blend them . .

T. You so want to blend again with this deeper emotional part of yourself, but only on the condition that
you remain in control . .

C. Right . .

T. You seem to say you know it would be a very serious
risk and that . .

C. That I don't want to take it yet . .

T. Uh huh . . like one part of you has been kind of
exiled and you don't want it to return until you're sure
you can handle it . .

C. I have to be sure before I can . . I think, in time, my
mind will be stronger . . like my mind is still weak . .
but my heart is still there and I don't want my heart to
overtake my mind . . that's what I'm trying to say . .

T. Yes . . you were dominated by your heart and look
what happened . .

C. Right . .

T. Now your mind is in control and you're not going
to risk that control until you're pretty sure . . but you do
want your heart back too . .

C. Yes . . I want to put my whole heart into the
things I do . .

T. But only when you're sure you still control what
you do . .

C. I feel pretty good sayin' what I did 'cause that
answered it . .

T. It gave you a clear picture of what you feel . .

So did a metaphor emerge from my efforts to contact an openly
disorganized female client. The metaphor clarified the transition
from one stage of our relationship to another. It clarified the transition
from modified encounter in her pathological world to the possibility
of congruent encounter in the real world. That clarity was a bridge
between us:

C. At first you acted like you seemed to understand how the lights were in my eyes . . now you act like you don't understand . .

T. At first I guess I sort of entered a little more into that world with you, Bonnie . . and I think maybe we understood each other there a little bit . . (pause) . . now I guess I'm saying . . I'm going to stay on the shore and hope you will come up onto the shore with me . . (pause) . .

C. Like that song, "My Bonnie Lies Over the Ocean," huh? . .

T. Yes, you lie way over the ocean in a foreign land someplace . . I guess I'm just going to wait for you here . . (pause) . .

I value such metaphor communication because it demands cognitive and emotional participation. A metaphor can be constructed only upon the cognitive and emotional impact of a phenomenon. A vital metaphor does demand an intuitive involvement in the referent experience. Yet metaphorical language is limited. It points to a phenomenon, but is not a *direct* experience of that phenomenon. I can construct a metaphor which will describe my fear. I risk much more by a *direct* encounter with that fear. The metaphor is thus a mode of partial encounter. The danger of such a mode is that it can readily become a digression from critical experience rather than a directive to it. The metaphor can become an abortive substitute for direct participation in the referent phenomenon itself. The illusion of encounter provided by the partial metaphor experience then becomes a substitute for the intended direct encounter. The possibility of such digression is inherent in the use of metaphorical language. It must be avoided in psychotherapy. I want to further explore here the contribution of authentic metaphor participation.

As a client, I want to make contact with the therapist. I cannot deal directly with him or therapy would no longer be necessary. We would rather be colleagues or companions involved in direct reciprocal communication. My goal and the goal of the therapist may be such direct communication. The problem then is not the goal, but the method to attain that goal. The indirect language of metaphors may be one useful approach.

Client and therapist must meet. Should they meet in a partial encounter, it can serve as a bridge to direct encounter. Should they recognize each other on the outskirts of town, they may walk home together. But the border terrain of interpersonal encounter is dark and irregular. There are no straight lines. All the forms are tentative and curved. The shapes are fleeting and ambiguous. Contact must be made around corners and over archways. The abrupt dimensions of angularity would quickly disrupt the soft groping in the night. Metaphorical language is native to the territory. It is a language made for subtle implicit communication. Its vitality and its danger are in its tenuous suggestive form. It can elicit subtle nuances of experience which are roughly overrun by direct denotative assault. It can nourish delicate communication potentials which might be uprooted by a more direct approach. Yet it does introduce the inherent danger. Metaphorical communication may flounder in its own aesthetic futility. It may become a useless indulgence rather than a difficult step toward interpersonal reality.

Another example may further clarify the communication potential of the metaphor. The encounter to be described here did not develop in a formal therapeutic relationship. Yet the interpersonal process seems common to the therapy prototype.

I wanted to know someone better and felt he wanted to know me. He was an older and more experienced person than myself. I was the more active participant in our interaction. We both knew our relationship was at an impasse. All our attempts to meet were dominated either by my cognitive or by my emotional participation. The dominant of these two modes consistently eclipsed the other. We met only in distorted forms. Cognitive and emotional participation merged in the metaphor communication. We met each other now as integrated selves. We were both present for the first time. We were tentative and distant, but we were there.

I had seen the man I wanted to know interact with a group of his students prior to our metaphor encounter. That interaction sequence was the referent experience for the metaphor which was so helpful to our relationship.

A small group had gathered near the door to briefly continue the topic under discussion at the end of the class. The group seemed genuinely involved in the topic. The emotional involvement apparently attracted his attention. He approached the edge of the group and made cautious hesitant gestures toward joining it. The group was so involved that no one noticed these tentative gestures. To avoid any intrusion which might disrupt the tenor of the group, he recovered suddenly and sidled quickly out the door.

This event made an impression on me. It touched me more and more as I reminisced about it. This mature man reacted to the subtlety of that situation with the sensitivity of a timid child. I was struck by an image. It was the proverbial elephant who is sensitive and vulnerable in spite of his power. The impact of the experience was in the nervous risk which was implicit in his reaction. It seemed the more mature a man became, the more sensitive and animated was his response to life. It seemed maturity had not brought comfortable stereotypes but enriched experiential vitality.

The image lingered with me. It was very much alive when we met again. I cautiously approached the metaphor by a discussion of my fondness for elephants. It was not so much an apologetic preparation for the metaphor comparison as an exploration of the metaphor terrain. The dimensions of the situation must be right. A metaphor cannot survive in a small space. An elephant needs room.

The other seemed to move gently with me into my discussion of animals. A hushed ambiguity settled over everything. A process began. Forms and shapes changed. Old dimensions merged into new ones. Angular forms became soft curves. Rough surfaces became smooth. Adamant shapes began to flow. A tentative suspended reality encompassed us both. An elephant emerged out of the dusk. He knew him: ". . an elephant who does a little dance." We met in our common encounter with the elephant. The metaphor was our occasion to experience interpersonal nuances which could not yet be directly expressed. The sensitivity of the other man was introduced into our relationship before we could directly approach it. The metaphor enabled us to share an awareness of his sensitive and vulnerable self. Reaching toward each other would be a risk for both of us. He was a person too! The work was yet to be done. The metaphor encounter was only a beginning; but it *was* a beginning.

The metaphor is thus a useful ancillary mode, but primary encounters demand much more than such partial participation. They demand direct and complete involvement by both participants. They demand a risk and a commitment more critical than metaphor experience can provide. A primary encounter must be a personal communication which comes to life in the moment and endures beyond it. An encounter which would not make a relationship vital in the lived world beyond the moment is not an authentic encounter. Only such genuine commitment by both participants can make a relationship real. All else is doomed to the failure inherent in any dishonest venture.

The metaphors cited here were not used as ends in themselves. They were not used as aesthetic constructs. They were used rather as bridges to direct encounter. As such, metaphorical language may be useful in psychotherapy.

Chapter 7
The Emergent Encounter

Relationship I (Hospitalized Female)

I knew that she was critically alone. I knew that she was torn loose from herself and from the real world. I knew her behavior would be broken and disjoint. I knew she would not come to me. I knew I must enter the chaos of her life.

I wanted no rules. I wanted only my own congruence. I sank into the interaction between us. A process of participation emerged. It began when we met on the ward. She looked directly into my face and whispered, "I have X-ray eyes." I answered, "X-ray me." She ran off, giggling with laughter. Therapy began two days later.

C. Oh, a recording machine, how about that . . safer that way, isn't it? . . (giggling laughter) . .

T. You think I do it to be on the safe side? . .

C. Yeah, I get around so much, huh . .

T. If we get it . .

C. (Giggling laughter) . .

T. On there exactly the way it happens it will be safer . .

C. Yeah . . (giggling laughter) . . (pause) . .

T. You know I think it's going to be sort of a struggle for me to get to know you . .

C. We going to have pretty pictures or somethin'? . .

T. It's not going to be easy . . 'cause I think you're pretty complicated . .

C. Yeah, I'm really complicated . . didn't start out that way, but that's the way I ended up . .

T. I guess we all start out pretty easy to understand but . .

C. Do I see pretty things and end up smellin' flowers over there? . .

T. You do . .

C. No I just walk past them . .

T. Outside . .

C. Yeah . . (pause) . . when's the jury trial? . .

T. There's a trial coming up . .

C. I don't know . . (pause) . . (paces around the

room, tearful and angry) . . I don't like nurses and
doctors either . .

T. I know . .

C. Yeah, I know you know . . and I'm tired of having
all those God damn lousy recordings in my head . .

T. I feel I really . .

C. (Sitting down again, now quiet and tearful) . . Oh,
it's not damn you . . it's the damn hospital that's all . .
(pause) . . can you see what's in my eyes? . .

T. I see tears in your eyes . .

C. Well, I see lights and things flyin' and codes and
everything else . . green lights, red lights, gold lights,
silver lights . .

T. I guess you wish there were just tears, but there are
so many other things too . .

T. (Later in the same first interview) . . I guess while
you've been talking I've been wondering if you ever
feel . . feel close to people . .

C. Sometimes I think they're inside me . . they can
smell my insides or somethin' . . like last night I had
gas in my stomach and it smelled like manure . .

T. People really do get close to you . . they get right
inside you . .

C. Yeah . .

T. That's closer than most people let anyone get . .

C. This is the funny farm, isn't it? . . they're goin' to
turn you into a bunch a little animals, aren't they? . .
I can talk to anything looks like . . (giggling laughter) . .

T. You can talk to anyone and anything . .

C. But I don't know what they say though . .

T. What they say back to you . .

C. Yeah . . who do you think you are, my mother? . .
who do you think you are, my father? . . who do you
think you are, my sister? . . who do you think you are,
my brother? . . everybody's switched around up there,
out there, in there . .

T. They keep switchin' . . that makes it tough . .

C. And I get crunchin' in my head like a stapler . .
and there's telephones in my head . .

T. You have the whole works, don't you? . .

C. And things flyin' through my brain . . and I can feel
aches and pains and . .

T. Anything goin' on now? . . I'd like to get in on some
of that . .

C. Oh, you would, huh? . . you think we really got somethin' goin' here . .

T. Yeah . . I'd like to get in on it 'cause I'm still just plain . .

C. Does it look like you write hot checks? . .

T. It does to you . .

C. I looked at a book one time about medicine and hallucinatin' drugs . . schizophrenic dual personality . .

T. All that stuff . . now you're gettin' in on all that . .

C. Oh, am I really? . . I don't want any reward . . I just want to go home . .

T. I know . . (pause) . .

C. Do we take each other's minds when we're in this little room? . .

T. I know I'd like to exchange a little mind stuff with you . .

C. You would . . it keeps comin' back . . they don't want me to get well . .

T. I see . .

C. (Toward the end of the same first interview) . . I looked at a magazine and I went into the women's room and a colored woman knifed me in the back . . and I went to see my son once and somethin' burst in here . . and . .

T. Your body just gets punished all the time . .

C. This is the agony ward isn't it? . . I seen purple and I saw a black coffin and . .

T. It sure is an agony ward . .

C. It happened at home too . .

T. I see . . (pause) . . I don't know how you feel . . but . . I'm glad that you're here with me now . .

C. (Tearful) . . They say I can bring back the dead and all that kind of jazz . . I can do this and I can do that . . now my eyes are floating . .

T. They just don't leave you alone . .

C. No . . they think I'm Santa Claus or somethin' . . I saw somethin' that looked like Christ in my sleep one night . . course it's all distorted now, I guess . . but he was real handsome and he looked angry, but he was clean shaven and had long rich gold hair and his eyes glowed and had lights in them . .

The second interview was important because there was a period of prolonged emotional contact between us. The contact persisted in spite of gaps in the logical dialogue. I held one of her hands and then the other during the interaction. I looked straight into her eyes when at all possible:

C. And that woman over there's telling fortunes . . she really can tell fortunes . . and I think I'm in Tijuana or somethin' . . I can see people checkin' hubcaps . . they're dressed-up so must be detectives or somethin' . . anyway those cops are big jokers . . we'll show her monsters . . am I callin' doctors and police monsters . . is that how they got me fixed up . . (pause) . . I think you're a flirt too, aren't you? . . (laughter) . .

T. You think I may be doin' some of that too, huh . .

C. I had a pretty bracelet once . .

T. You know I would like to get close to you . .

C. Do you think I smell like a mouse? . .

T. I don't smell you, but I wouldn't give a damn what you smelled like . .

C. Anyway I'm losin' my sense of smell . . I don't go around smellin' people, but it's where I live, I can't help it . . I just turn around and whoever's in my eyes can smell, huh . . anyway . . (pause) . . I felt another presence . .

T. Someone else . .

C. Uh huh . . I can't tell if she's sympathy or what . . maybe she's mad . . (pause) . . (laughter) . . (pause) . . now they're prayin' or doin' heathen or somethin' . . (pause) . . you read your own mind in my eyes too? . .

T. I'm just enjoying you . .

C. You're with somebody else . . (pause) . . you recording over there too? . . (pause) . . I think I oughta put some marks on my arms . . (pause) . . (angry and tearful) . . you better quit that . .

T. My just looking at you is difficult for you . .

C. (Tearful) . . I have too many faces . . too many laughin' . . (pause) . . you cryin' for me too? . .

T. I'd like to cry with you . . (I took one of her hands in both of mine) . .

C. (Sigh) . . You see, I got everything tuned in now . . (pause) . . they say they oughta get six months in jail for that . . looks like that guy said he seen me with a priest on television . . (pause) . . what do you feel in this hand now? . . should I take off that ring? . . (I held her other hand) . .

T. No, that's all right . . this hand doesn't feel quite as warm . . (pause) . . now it does . . now it's beginning to feel warm . .

C. Some people see different things in them . . sometimes they see God or Jesus . .

T. I come closer to seeing you here than I have . . (pause) . .

C. Are you an atheist? . .

T. I believe in you . .

C. Why . . because you have to believe in yourself, huh? . .

T. I believe in myself and in you . . (pause) . .

C. You think you can bring me back to normal by that? . .

T. Sometimes believing in someone . .

C. I have a technician in my teeth (opens her mouth) . . see, up here . .

T. You have very pretty teeth . . I don't see the things in them you do . .

C. And I'm a big hypocrite and I change all the time, huh? . .

T. I don't know that part of you . . I've only seen you two times here and one time over there . . and all I've ever seen is someone who seems very unhappy . .

C. Aren't you seein' the whole ward in your eyes . . they're all sendin' you messages . .

T. I could probably get in on all that but right now I'm concerned just about you . .

C. Now it said, "Don't you recognize my presence?" . . who's that supposed to be . . and there's telephone calls constantly goin' on . .

T. I know . . I wish they'd all hang up and leave us alone . .

C. They don't do it though . .

T. Maybe they will . .

C. 'Cause everybody's got a goin' thing in this hospital, huh? . .

T. Yeah . . but maybe we can cut 'em out though . .

The next excerpt is from the fourth interview. It was important because for the first time she tried to deal with the images and voices as a part of her own personal struggle for her own personal identity and not as forces external to her and beyond her control. I took her face in my hands and looked into her eyes near the beginning of the interaction to let her know that I was there since recognition of my presence seemed so confused and limited:

C. Now do you see a businessman in my eyes or is he a minister or somethin'? . .

T. I just see you . . (pause) . . I just see you . .

C. It says, "God damn you, shut up!" . . 'cause they fixed me up in a religious way once and somebody messed that up . .

T. You got pretty close to religion and someone ruined that? . .

C. No . . I was fightin' with my husband . . and he was threatening my life . . runnin' through the house . . and I got mad at the police . . and the police was always comin' over there . . and . .

T. Now look, Bonnie . .

C. You want me to forget that, huh? . .

T. No, I don't mind you talking like that . . I'm just sayin' it's tough as hell for me to sit here and talk with you and not really feel you here . .

C. Oh, you feel me here, I get a little thrill in my stomach and in my chest . . does that mean I'm afraid of you or I'm a whore? . . my trouble is I'm too hard-headed, huh? . . boy, they're clankin' now . .

T. (I stood up, held her face in my hands, and looked into her eyes) . . I just want to touch you gently to let you know I'm here . .

C. (Voice tender and hushed). . Sounded for a minute you thought my skin was meltin' and I looked horrible . .

T. No, you just feel soft and warm . .

C. Men do say I'm comfortable . . my husband used to think that somebody was comin' up to the house so he'd be late for work watchin', but no one ever came so he went to work . . anyway they talked like he went to work . . one time I didn't have any blankets on me so my brother-in-law put the blankets on me . . my husband's brother is in prison and I used to write to him and we used to talk about the records we liked . . I had a lot of fun in my life, believe it or not . . I was kind of wild but . . so if I do die like someone's tryin' to say . . well that's just tough . .

T. There were times when you felt close with people and if you should die now . . you've had some of life anyway . .

C. You didn't think so, did you? . .

T. You think I felt you just never had anything at all . .

C. You thought I just went out and prostituted myself . . looks like I do all kinds of things, but Sally Jane's the one that shaves and looks like atomic stuff's coming out her bottom . . and she's always pickin' at her bottom and her privates like I do when I pick my nose . .

T. I see . .

C. And when I go to the bathroom, I see somebody's face down there once in a while . . I didn't used to, but just before I came here I thought sausage links was comin' out of me so I was in touch with it then . .

T. But, before all those things started happening, you did have some nice times in your life . .

C. Oh, definitely . .

T. You had some people I guess you did trust . .

C. Oh yes . . you see that's my trouble . . I trusted everybody . .

T. And when you've been really hurt by trusting people then you just don't want to trust anyone anymore . . (pause) . .

C. "Gee, Bonnie, looks like you're the President or somethin', huh?" . . that's what somebody's thinkin' . . did you get that message? . . I played that record that's why they put me in here . . detectives and ministers and cops all flyin' at my house all the time . . (pause) . .

T. You know, a feeling I had just a moment ago was that I was standing between you and all that noise . . and they couldn't get through . . and I felt for just a moment that we were alone . .

C. We're never alone . . (slight laugh) . .

T. I felt it for just a moment and I liked it . .

C. How did you feel? . .

T. That we were alone . . just the two of us . .

C. In bed, huh? . .

T. I would like to be in bed with you alone but . .

C. You mean physically anyway, don't you? .. I mean mentally . . they say everybody's doin' it . .

T. Because I've felt the warmth of you, I would like to feel that warmth in bed . . but I don't think that's the way we can do it here . .

C. Now the bottom half's turnin' over . . how about that . . what'd I see there . .

T. I hope you didn't see anything but me . .

C. Maybe it's in my head anyway . . sounded like it said, "You leave my mama alone." . .

T. He's trying to protect you . .

C. You look somethin' like my stepfather . . that's why I laugh . . because everybody's disguised different around here . .

T. I just see you . .

C. I bet . .

T. I'm looking right at you now and I see just you . .

C. You have a mirror and you're lookin' at yourself, that's all . .

T. I'm looking right at you and I'm seeing you . . somewhere way down inside your eyes . . I can see you . .

C. You're hypnotizing me now, huh? . .

T. I don't know . . my eyes water a little . . part with tears because it's sad how difficult it is for us and how mixed-up it all is . .

C. You're talkin' to someone else . .

T. I'm talking to you . . I'm telling you I'm sad . .

C. You're talking to someone else . . that's what a voice said anyway . .

T. Sometimes they're liars . . I'm talking to you . .

C. The Bible said everybody's goin' to have a number . . now they're tryin' to turn us into mechanical minds, huh? . .

T. I had another feeling . . (pause) . . that you could give so much to your son who needs you . .

C. They're tryin' to use me now . .

T. I just want to be close to you . . I don't want to use you for anything . .

C. They're comin' to get me now . .

T. I don't think so yet . . that's one of those false ones in there . . (pause) . . (moves chair up very close) . . you're being so nice and quiet I want to get a little closer to enjoy being with you . .

C. Anyway, I'm the funniest girl they ever saw . .

T. You give 'em one big laugh? . .

C. I guess so . . (pause) . . is that your thought? . . (laughs) . . yeah, you're laughin' all right (laughs) . .

T. You know maybe they think you're funny . .

C. You're a comedian too, aren't you? . .

T. You know they think you're so funny . .

C. That's why they keep revivin' me and can't kill me, huh? . .

T. Just to have you around for laughs . . (pause) . . you aren't funny to me . . you worry me and make me afraid . .

C. Because I don't scream at monsters, huh? . .

T. Because you seem so alone . . (pause) . .

C. And I don't go around screwin' dogs either . .

T. I know . .

C. And I don't screw hairbrushes and I'm not . . now it feels like I got a pig in my head . . and I seen a big silver thing one time and it had a woman screwin' around with a donkey . .

T. All that is possible . .

C. And a girl told me about a grapefruit . .

T. It's possible for you to do all those things . .

C. You're a mind reader all right. .

T. It's possible to do all those things you think about . .

C. (Emphatic) . . I don't think about them . . that's just what they tell me and what I hear . .

T. I see . . but it's possible to do all those things . . it's possible you've done them . .

C. And everything we think about and what everybody else thinks about looks like its done to us, huh? . .

T. But a person has to decide what is real for them . . and you say that screwin' hairbrushes . .

C. (Abrupt) . . Oh . . and you think I screw around with my son too . . well I never have . .

T. There's another thing . . and they say you do this . . now are you tellin' me straight—you do or you don't? . .

C. Well . . I've seen my mother doin' weird things too, but she hasn't done them . .

T. She didn't really . .

C. Screw a door . . I don't screw a door . .

T. But you've seen pictures and think maybe it could happen . . your mother screw a door or you screw a door . .

C. Yeah . .

T. But you never screwed your son or are you just tellin' me that? . .

C. No . . I definitely never screwed my son . . one

time he put his hand down there . . I used to sleep with
him and he put his hand down there in his sleep and I
moved it away . .

T. He just wanted to be close to you in bed and maybe
you wanted him close . .

C. No, I didn't . . so then I started sleeping during
the day and staying awake at night . .

T. You didn't want to have sex with your boy . .

C. And he didn't ever ask me to and I didn't ever ask
him to . .

T. You didn't want that out in the open . . that you
might want to have sex with each other . .

C. No . . definitely . . I am fixed up altogether different than I was fixed up on the outside . . I was afraid of
lightning shootin' in my house and I put on a dress to go
out and I took my son with me most of the time and . .

T. You know, I used to worry about having sex with
my mother . .

C. You know, the Bible brings a lot of filth into people's
minds . .

T. It got you thinking about sex with your boy . .

C. (Emphatic) . . No, it did not . . it was somebody
else's thought mirrored through my brain . . that was
their mind, not my mind . . I never once even thought
of it . .

T. Well, in my mind I'm telling you I have . . I thought
of sex with my mother . . in my own mind and nobody put it there . . I thought of it and it worried me
. . it worried me a lot . .

C. Well it sounds like I want to have sex with my father,
brother, or somethin', but I haven't . .

T. So these could be thoughts you have . .

C. And I was always scared of sex until my sister told
me it was all right if you love someone . .

T. I see . . and if you'd really been in love . .

C. And if you could hear Dr. _____ 's recordings . .
if he made any . . they'd be altogether different . .

T. Maybe our relationship is a little different . .

C. You know him? . .

T. I just want to know you . .

C. Anyway, I was scared and tense and I'd sit up in
his chair . . and I was afraid of colored people . .
and I'd sit up in the chair . . and then one night,
"Mama, that's not me," and he thought I saw it but I
didn't . . and I'd wish for a telephone and I'd see a

telephone in my eyes . . and I could see a little hand comin' up like that and I put on a dress and electricity started shootin' through it so I ripped it off . . and somebody's been feedin' everybody a bunch of bull about me because I haven't done nothin' compared to what they're doin' to my mind sayin', "Take her to Tijuana" . . I went once to Tijuana with my hus . . my so . . see . .

T. It's getting mixed-up again . .

C. (Emphatic) . . With my husband . . he's seen a lot and he wouldn't take me with him . . they tied a woman to a tree and all had intercourse with her . . it wasn't me, but it probably looked like it was me . .

T. Again all that sex stuff is possible . . it's possible to screw animals . . it's possible to screw your father, your brother, your son . . it's all possible . . it's possible for me to screw my mother . . if I had a sister, I could screw her . .

C. Well my sister was in a girl's school and so she had me feel her breasts and it disgusted me . .

T. I see, sometimes sex stuff gets mixed up between girls too . . it is possible for girls to have sex with girls . . it's possible for men to have sex with men . . I've known a lot of queers . . even been close to some . . but I said, "I'd rather fuck women" . .

C. Yes, I know . . Judy stuck her finger up me one time and I told her I preferred a man . .

T. I see . . you just clearly said: "Okay, so you can finger-fuck me, but I'd rather have a man do it" . . you made a decision . . you said: "I'd rather have a man fuck me" . . these are just decisions everyone has to make . .

C. I think you're talking to someone on the telephone . .

T. I'm just talking to you right here . .

C. The heck you are . .

T. I'm just talking to you about you wonderin' about screwin' your son, and your brother, and the girl finger-fucking you, and feelin' the girl's breasts . . all the things you've got to work through and decide about . .

C. You tryin' to give me a climax or somethin' . . can't have climaxes in your head, can you? . .

T. You can have all kinds of climaxes between people . . climaxes of love and affection . . we don't have to really fuck each other to have climaxes . .

C. Is that why you wear a rubber? . .

T. No, I'm not wearing any . . I don't think we have to worry about babies . . the kind of climaxes we might have . .

C. Like we're sittin' on the bed talkin' . .

T. We're just sittin' here lookin' at each other and talkin' to each other . .

C. Now you're really goin' to cuss me out when you play that back . . you'd like to slap my face now, wouldn't you? . .

T. (I reached over slowly and touched her face gently with my hand) . . That's all I want to do . . touch you gently . .

C. I get embarrassed . . that's why I laugh . .

T. I see . . it's easier sometimes to laugh . .

C. Like my girlfriend, Judy . . she laughs when she's embarrassed . .

T. Yes, there's a kind of embarrassed laughter . . people giggle sometimes under tension . . (pause) . . I guess it would be less embarrassing if someone did slap you rather than just touch you gently . .

C. I better go back to the ward now, huh? . .

T. You think it's time to go? . .

C. Don't you? (laughs) . .

T. It probably is about time, but otherwise I'd like to talk to you for a long while yet . . (pause) . .

C. What kind of a mind you got anyway? (laughs) . .

T. Almost as funny as yours, I guess . .

C. I guess so . . I feel I'm hot . . how about that, got hot and now I have to go back to the ward . .

T. Part of being close may be that you do get worked up that way . .

C. I was readin' a story once and somebody inside my head said, "Gee I'm hot," and I got hot myself . .

T. Uh huh . . you do get feeling that way sometimes when you get close to another person . .

C. Now I got a pain in my leg . . I heard somethin' down there say they'd like to break that leader in my leg, huh? . .

T. Now it's those kind of things I'd like to push out of here so that they don't interrupt you all the time . . (pause) . . and I'm sort of damned if I'm not going to get close to you . . you're going to have to push me away awfully hard if you don't want me around . .

C. You want me to push you away? . .

T. No, I want to stay close to you . .

C. Someone else wants that . . someone's really getting some information, huh? . .

The preceding excerpt from the fourth interview was the turning point of the first phase of therapy. The client continued to be actively disorganized during the fifth interview, but leveled off during the sixth and seventh sessions. The eighth of these daily one-hour interviews was clearly the beginning of a new phase of therapy. She was subdued, depressed, and moved at a much slower pace. She was even difficult to recognize emotionally:

C. I seem to get worse off instead of better . .

T. It seems that way to you . . just getting worse, not better . . (pause) . .

C. Now my temples are real tense and so is my throat . .

T. Uh huh . . feels tight around your eyes and in your throat . . (pause) . .

C. If it wasn't for my boy, I think I'd just like to shoot myself . .

T. If you didn't have your love for him, maybe there'd be nothing, and you just might as well end it all suddenly . . (pause) . .

C. (Later in the same eighth interview) . . You wouldn't want to be locked up, would you? . .

T. I guess in my life there have been times . . when it might have seemed best for a while . .

C. Yeah . . is that why you went into psychiatry? . .

T. You're wondering if maybe I'm concerned about people who have troubles because I've had troubles myself . .

C. Everybody's got problems . . (pause) . . I'd just like to know what's going on inside my head . .

T. You would like to understand what it's all about a little better . .

C. Uh huh . . (pause) . . I hate to be locked up . .

T. I know . .

C. (Tearful) . . I just feel like I'm some kind of a mechanical toy or somethin' with all this goin' on in my head . .

T. You just feel you're not a person at all . .

C. Not any more . .

T. You're just a mechanical robot with tears in her eyes . . (pause) . . and you struggle so hard to keep those tears from really flowing . . (pause) . .

C. (Near the end of the same eighth interview) . . At first, you acted like you seemed to understand how the lights were in my eyes . . and now you act like you don't understand . .

T. At first, I guess I sort of entered a little more into that world with you, Bonnie . . and I think maybe we understood each other there a little bit . . (pause) . . now, I guess I'm saying . . I'm going to stay on the shore and hope you will come up onto the shore with me . . (pause) . .

C. Like that song, "My Bonnie Lies Over the Ocean," huh? . .

T. Yes, you lie way over the ocean in a foreign land someplace . . I guess I'm just going to wait for you here . . (pause) . .

The first phase of therapy took place in her bizarre experiential world. We met and understood each other there. The next phase of therapy must take place in the real world. It is my hope that this first meeting will be the bridge to our second.

No pattern was forced on our relationship. Yet a pattern of interaction did emerge. I was empathic when the client was emotionally engaged in the relationship. I reached toward her with my own emotional participation when I could not feel her present. I entered actively into her bizarre experiential world when I felt an encounter was possible there. I met her in the experience of common metaphors. I touched her body with my own when such a movement emerged from my deepest congruent self. It was not a process imposed on the relationship. It was rather a process which emerged out of the relationship itself. It was responsive enough to encompass a wide range of diverse interaction.

Relationship II (Hospitalized Male)

He was only nineteen years old. Yet already he had climbed near to Heaven—then been dashed to Hell. He had been a Hindu monk in India. He reached spiritual heights which intoxicated him; he could not contain himself; he fell. He was returned to this country severely disorganized. I met him on a hospital ward six months later. I will let him tell you the rest:[1]

---

[1] The interaction sequences which follow were taken from a series of recorded excerpts published by the Tape Library of the American Academy of Psychotherapists (Tape 39).

(This is from the first in a series of daily one-hour interviews)

C. (Long silence) . . I guess you could say . . a . . I . . I don't know what's the matter with me . . and I . . I don't know why you sit there and don't say anything . .

T. And that's what you mean . . it's up to me . . I should heal you . . I should know the right words to say . . I should know what's wrong with you . .

C. Yeah . . yeah . .

T. And tell you . .

C. Yeah . .

T. And when I sit here quietly and say nothing . . you wonder . . is he keeping it from me or . .

C. Yeah . .

T. Uh huh . .

C. (Pause) . . And I . . I feel that you don't like me . .

T. I see . . my silence means to you . . that I don't like you . .

C. Yeah . .

T. Because, if I liked you, I would tell you more and explain more to you . .

C. Yeah . . (pause) . . I mean . . if I could only . . if you could put me in hypnosis or something . . if I could tell you how it happened . . now if you could see a film of it or something . . I'll tell you one thing . . before I went into the hospital . . a . . I had this dream . . and . . could I have a piece of paper and a pencil? . . (goes over to desk) . .

T. You're welcome to anything you can find there . .

C. (Sits on floor in front of T. with paper and pencil) . . Here's how it was . . this is the picture (draws abstract figures while talking) . . this is love in America . . this is myself . . and these are the vultures in India . . these are the ones that cut my heart out . . now here are guys on surfboards and this is the ocean . . it's very cold out here . . here I am leaving America . . this is a very simultaneous thing . . and I'm paddling toward a religion to find my soul . . and, right here, I find in the religion, vultures . . (T. Hmm . . hmm) . . it all happened because I was at this temple here . . this is called "Gondal" . . and because I didn't study Gujarati . . the language . . there's where I got hurt . . right here, by Swamigee . . and I went to this temple . .

this is called "Aksharban," and I . . as a result of my not studying, my mind was loose and I . . the food got to me . . when you're a missionary, you're not supposed to take rough foods . . so I went here . . and here I was hurt . . (draws black circular scribbles all over paper) . . again and again and again and again and round and round and round and round . .

T. So the first hurt . . here . . sort of weakened you . . and then when you reached here it . .

C. Yeah . . this is where the confusion started . . that's how I am now . . I don't know what's wrong . . all I remember is coming down these stairs . . I went over here . . and I walked down the stairs and looked over here . . and my teacher was getting ready to go . . I was sick here, upstairs . . I had fever, jaundice, and dysentery . . and I went up and looked at him and he just gave me the coldest meanest thing I've ever had . . it just . . wow . . and in this dream they were black, and it was sort of a cornfield . . and it was dark and there were vultures . . just vultures . .

T. And this is where the vultures really fed on you . . right here . .

C. Yeah . . right here . .

T. And just one person stabbed you first . .

C. Yeah . .

T. Then everyone got eating on you . .

C. Yeah . .

T. Uh huh . .

C. (Got up from floor onto his chair again) . . Yeah . . and I wasn't strong . .

T. That's right . . you say you were weakened by the diet and by the lack of study and lack of discipline . . but then the thing that really cut you was his look . .

C. Yeah . .

T. And his rejection . . and from then on, I guess, you've been sort of lost and damaged and hurt, day after day . .

C. I'm so lost . . I just got this . . it hurts in my heart *very bad* . . it feels like my heart is just tied around with wire and there's a big thorn there . .

I struggled with only limited success to contact him during the second and third hours. Then a significant encounter emerged abruptly during the fourth session:

C. I'll probably see Dr. _____ this afternoon . . I wonder if he'll let me go for a visit . . you know he can change his mind . . he can slap me . . he can step on me . . he can break my thumbs . . he can do anything he wants because I'm his little patient here . . (pause) . . and it's not funny . .

T. I know it's not . . but for some reason the way you say it . . it is (laughs) . .

C. Well . . it's funny for you . . but it's not funny for me . .

T. It is for you . . you're laughing too . .

C. (Laughs) Oh, hell . .

T. And this is what's wrong with it . . the real pain doesn't come through . . it's choked off, just like the tears and the laughter . .

C. (Abrupt) . . The thorn is right here . . (points to his chest) . .

T. And it's choked in there . . choked real tight . . and you can even smile when you say you're getting stepped on . . you're getting kicked . .

C. (Laughs) . .

T. See we can laugh about it . . and the . .

C. Let me go try to get a cigarette . . would you mind . .

T. (Intense laugh) . . Right in the middle of my statement . . see how uninvolved you are . . you're talkin' about this and thinkin' about that . . just when I'm trying to get through to you . .

C. (Intense laugh) . .

T. Through that wall . . that wall . . it's lead . . it's the hardest lead I ever saw (laughs) . .

C. (Laughs) . . See, I told you . .

T. I know (laughs) . .

C. It's a hell of a mix, man . .

T. I know . .

C. That's why I like my sister and her husband . .

T. They get through it somehow . .

C. They're like you . . you're a good man . . you remind me of a human being . .

T. (Laughs) . . I just vaguely remind you of one . . you're not sure . . (intense laughter both C. and T.) . . oh, John . . oh . . I don't know, John . .

C. (Intense laugh) I wish you'd come to Palm Springs with me . . we could have a party at my sister's house . .

T. I'd like to come . . I've been down there a couple

of times . . it's real nice down there . .

C. Oh, man . .

T. This time of year it really . .

C. (Abrupt) . . But the thorn's still there . .

T. Even down there . . you're going to take it with you . . yeah, you can't . . the sunshine isn't going to melt that out . . that's my feeling . . that only by going down into yourself can you loosen this thing and let it flow out . .

C. (Abrupt) . . All right . . I'll start right now . . (pause) . . I made love to a woman and I became like her in body and form and thinking and everything . . and that's why I don't feel loved by you . . is because I feel that I'm an Indian woman . .

T. (Soft) . . I see . .

C. After I left my master I went and surrendered to a woman . . which was sex . . see, I wasn't allowed to have sex when I was in the temple . . and so my soul was brought up to such a degree . . whereas I was obeying and trying to be like my teacher . . and when I went to the woman and got a piece of ass from her, that's when my soul changed to hers . .

T. (Soft) . . I see . .

C. So this is the pool of blood that exists within me . .

T. (Soft) . . You became a woman and lost your manhood . .

C. Hmm . .

T. (Soft) . . And you haven't recovered from that yet . .

C. Yeah . .

T. (Soft) . . And you think because of that I can't love you . .

C. Yeah . . it's . . yeah . . it's a terrible thing . . I'm really sought out . . I should just kill myself . .

Then we met in an even more intimate way during the fifth hour:

T. It seems today that you won't even think about last time . . (pause) . .

C. (Sigh) . . I don't know . .

T. (Soft) . . You told me some very personal things about yourself last time . .

C. (Pause) . . See, I don't know what's personal about myself . . I don't know what to tell you . . see, I'm so confused I don't know what to say . .

T. You don't feel the difference when you say something from deeper down inside . .

C. I don't know what's right and what's wrong . . I don't know what's kind and what isn't kind . .

T. Even what's you and not you . .

C. Yeah . . that's why I say, under hypnosis, I wouldn't know the difference between right and wrong . . I'd only know whatever comes out . . (pause) . . I'm not looking for hypnosis as an artificial way . . I just know that I won't be able to tell you the truth anymore . . I've told quite a lot . . more than I thought I would . .

T. And for some reason you're stopping . . you're calling it to a halt . .

C. It's stopping . . I'm not stopping it . . it's stopping . .

T. It's slowing down . . and somehow you say this *it* is not you . .

C. Well, it would be under hypnosis . . see because . .

T. I feel it might be you because you take it into your hands and say . . "This is me!" . .

C. Uh huh . .

T. And that's going to take a lot of real courage on your part . . to say . . "This is me!" . . come what may . .

C. Yeah . . (long pause) . . see, I'm a very holy person . . and divine . . (T. Uh huh) . . I was pure at heart and I only loved what was true . . (T. Uh huh) . . and I only loved my teacher . . I loved nothing else . . and I couldn't have sex but I didn't desire it . . I believe I'm like Jesus Christ but in a different way . . I mean the coming of Jesus Christ as it says in the Bible isn't exactly the way he's going to come . . he comes in a different way . . through a different religion . . through Hinduism . .

T. So you feel that you might be involved in this in some way . .

C. Yes . . very much . . I feel that I'm involved in a great religious thing . . and I was in India . . and it broke off . . that's what I'm unhappy about . . that's why I don't like to go back to work and back to the ward because those are the wrong places . . I need to be straightened out here . . I need to tell you some very vital things . .

T. The words all came out then . . but you're not sure how real they felt . .

C. No . . just the last second about what I have to go back to and stuff . .

T. Up to that point it was real . .

C. It was very real . . true . . completely . .

T. That you were involved in the kind of religious destiny you had been seeking . .

C. *Uh huh* . .

T. Then suddenly you were cut off from it . .

C. *Uh huh* . .

T. And you haven't been right since then . . (pause) . . and someway you must get back to your deeper destiny . .

C. *Truth* . . (long pause) . . see, I was like Christ in a way . . I was . . very pure and truthful and I only wanted the pure God in my heart . . but when I couldn't study . . see my teacher told me that the pure God would come into my heart after I studied the language . . but since I didn't have good study habits . . well, I just didn't study it . . that's how I got all fouled up . .

T. All the things you'd been needing so deeply were coming true . . you were finding the inner purity you had so wanted . . then it all went bad . .

C. (Pause) . . See, I don't know exactly what you want from me . . but it seems like I told you just then . . I believed . . (heavy sigh) . . I don't know . . (pause) . . I believed that I'm . . I was the second coming of Christ . . and I was pure and good until my heart was broken . .

T. (Soft) . . I see . . you feel that you were the new beginning for man . .

C. Yes . . I was the new religious upliftment . .

T. And just as you were really growing into that . . you got cut off . .

C. Hmm . . yes . . I was doing fine . . I understood as much as I could . . but my teacher said I wouldn't understand anymore until I study . . he said it would take six months . .

T. He put you this task . .

C. Yes . . he said, "Now if you obey me you'll have Darshon" . . Brahma Darshon . . that was like the seeing of Christ but a much more powerful seeing . . more than Christ . . big seeing . . you see God right

in the face . . and it takes learning the language . .
studying the language . .

T. I see . . so much was promised . . and then . .

C. I didn't think it was very important . . I was so
happy from what enlightenment I already had . . that
when he said . . study and then you'll know . . you'll
see completely . . (pause) . . but I didn't follow
through on it . . I didn't study . . so then he got mad
at me . .

T. You mean somehow you already felt you had
reached the vision and the goal you had been seeking . .

C. Yes . . well, I knew I didn't have the complete
Brahma Darshon . . or maybe I did . . but I was
just so happy and carefree . . you know . . I didn't
give a damn . .

T. Uh huh . . and when he put you another goal and
another step you said, "I don't really need those" . .

C. Well . . it was too much trouble . . I was so happy
that I didn't want to sit down and study . .

T. Uh huh . . you were living right in the midst of so
much inner joy . .

C. Oh, yes . . gee, was I happy . . boy, I was the
happiest man on earth . . (stretches out on the floor by
his chair) . . man . . (loud sigh) . . (pause) . . see,
I just didn't carry through on it . . I didn't have study
habits . . I remember when my teacher . . when he
gave me the books . . I said, "Swamigee, I don't have
study habits" . . and he just . . he didn't listen . .
(pause) . . and, another thing, he's supposed to be all
pure and right so I thought that when he didn't listen it
was right, you know . . but it's wrong . . he should
have listened . . he should have tried to talk to me real
silent and stuff . . either he should have talked to me
more or I should have talked to him . . he should have
understood that I didn't have good study habits and we
should have worked on it . . he should have talked to
me or something . .

T. Uh huh . . I see . . that in the perfection he had
reached . . he should have understood that . .

C. Yes . . (long pause) . . (T. sits down on floor next
to C.) . . Oh, I was so much like a religious man, like
Christ . . oh, I was so happy . . I had so much joy in
my new life living in India . . living like a saint . .

being a saint . . only pursuing God's love . . seeing
God . . see this Swamigee . . he was not like Christ
but more of Christ . . in India, there's Brahma . .
that means he's reached the total ultimate goal . . see
Brahma, and a Parabrahm . . over Brahma . . and
they have you know like church . . they have temple
. . and they have . . it's called an "archon" . . and
they have a candle they wave in front of it . . they have
these big idols of God . . and they go . . (C. began to
chant a lyrical Hindu sacrament . . I entered into the
mood with him . . we met in the intimacy of those
tender moments . . when the chant ended the communion between us lingered . . he looked directly at
me) . . I wonder . . what . . what do you think . .
of it . . all? . .
T. (Deeply personal and deeply committed) . . I think
. . you and I . . are going to be friends . .

I knew therapy had begun. We had been present to each other. Still
there was a long way to go. The work was yet to be done. We continued to meet daily for several more weeks. We had further experiences of interpersonal intimacy. Yet we could not go beyond the
level we had already attained. We were at an impasse. I tried to
break through that impasse during the twenty-third hour:

T. (Wandering around the room, staring at the walls,
standing in the corners) . . By me being the way I am
now . . just sort of not paying any attention to anything
and just not being here . . I'm not here now either . .
I'm over in the corner and I'm not gonna come out
until I'm ready . . and while I'm fooling around this
way you can get some idea of how . . how impossible
it is for me to make contact with you . . here I am
walkin' around . . foolin' around . . talking' and actin'
as if I know what's comin' off . . but I don't know
anything that's goin' on now . . I don't have any idea
what I'm doin' . .
C. You don't? . .
T. I see you sittin' there but I don't even know who you
are . . I haven't any idea who you are . .
C. I barely understand the expression you use . .
T. You know . . it doesn't matter . . 'cause it's much
more comfortable just letting everything go this way . .
C. For you . .

T. It is comfortable for me 'cause I'm tired . . and this kinda . . this kinda just lettin' go . . it really is comfortable . .

C. For you . . I don't blame you for being tired . . I got a big problem . .

T. Yeah . . letting things go like this is just more comfortable . . it leaves me with a sick feeling inside . . but I can just sit for a moment and say the hell with it . . and that's the way you lead your whole life . .

C. You think I can say the hell with it . . I'm stuck with it . .

T. You say the hell with it in terms of your deepest sickness . . You don't ever get down to that . .

C. I don't even know what it is . .

T. You see the difference is if I want to sink down all of a sudden into myself right now, I can . . I can really sink down and feel what I feel . . you can't . .

C. Everything's my fault . .

T. It's the fault of the sickness . . and the sickness is yours . . and I think that . .

C. Yeah . . it's mine . . I have it . . I belong with it . . it's my loving companion . .

T. Yes . . it is . . and you use it to hide behind and . .

C. Hide . .

T. And cover you up and so on . . yeah . . (pause) . .

C. I think your ego's gettin' at ya . . that's the trouble . .

T. What's happening to it? . .

C. My . . I'm so close to truth . .

T. Yes, you are . . you're close to some kind of crisis . . you're very close to it . .

C. Hmm . . yeah . . I just wish I wasn't alive . . if I wasn't here, then it'd be okay . .

T. But you are . . at least halfway . . and whatever part of you is still here, is here . . and we're goin' to have to try to see what that's all about . . but I think you are near collapsing and doing something crazy . . I'm sure of that . . aren't you? . .

C. (Laughter) . . I don't know what I'm doing . . something's happening . . I feel it . .

T. Yeah . . so do I . . and I don't know what . . what form it's goin' to take . . but it doesn't matter to me . . any form . . any form at all . . I don't care . . but something . .

C. Something . .

T. Yeah . .

C. Not this time . . but next time . . everything is a day away . .

T. Yeah . . I know it is . . sure . . the days drag on and . .

C. Shit . .

T. Before you know it you'll be . .

C. This old cactus is still thorny as hell . .

T. Yeah . . sure . . yeah . . you're still thirsty and dying . . but you won't . . you won't . . (pause) . .

C. (Laughter) . . You've got a problem too . . wanderin' around . . not thinking straight . .

T. I know . .

C. What the hell's the matter with you . .

T. Right now I have just the same kind of thing you have . . I just don't know what's going on . .

C. (Laughter) . . It's the truth . . you dumb fucker . . you don't know what you're doin' . .

T. I don't know what's happenin' . .

C. Shit . .

T. I'm completely out of it . . yeah . . but I don't mind . . it feels comfortable and I'm tired . . as I say . . it feels . . I don't mind it . . there's a kind of joy in this sort of sickness . . you had this kind of joy for a long time . . you were floatin' just all over the whole business . . you thought you were all right . . you thought this was happiness . . then all of a sudden the bottom fell out of it and you found you can't get along just floatin' around like this . . and I know better . . but I'm just floatin' for a moment . . for a little while 'cause I . .

C. I see some hope . . there is a hope . . I don't know where in the hell it came from . . but all the time during my sick crisis . . and Lord, you know, suffering . . you don't see it . . but now I do . . I did . . I saw something . . I don't . . I mean it's like I'm gonna be saved . .

T. Well . . I think you may be . . but I don't know yet how or when . .

C. Shit . . I don't either . . I tell you if there's this much shit and all that shit's cleared up . . there's gonna be a golden boy . . (pause) . . you might have here a prize heifer on your hands . . (laughter) . .

T. Yeah . . (pause) . . or an old fouled up pig . . I
think that's it . .

C. (Laughter) . . An old fouled up pig . . God damn
. . an old fouled up pig . . shit . . (laughter) . .

T. Yeah . . I wouldn't be surprised . . (pause) . .
I don't know if I can come back now . .

C. (Laughter) . . You better watch what you're doin'
. . you're goin' to start paintin' on the walls or somethin' . .

T. I know, and I really don't know if I can come back
. . I don't want to . . I don't want to come back to
the burden of you . .

C. Yeah . .

T. I just . . you know, I'd rather just sorta drift
around and just not have to be concerned about you . .

C. (Laughter) . . God damn psychologist playing
with the walls . . fuck . . what's the matter with you
. . someone see you doing that you're goin' to get
fired . .

T. Oh, well . .

C. (Laughter) . . I've never seen you like this before . .

T. You haven't, huh? . .

C. God damn . . you're actin' human . .

T. Hmm . . yeah . . it's possible for me to be as sorta
crazy as you are if I wanta be . .

C. Yeah . .

T. And to be as unhappy about it too . . I'm not . .
I'm not . .

C. You don't seem too happy now . .

T. I'm not havin' a good time . .

C. You look like you're sufferin' through me . .

T. I'm unhappy . .

C. Or with me . .

T. And not . . not really frightened·. . but a little bit
uneasy . . and . . and a little bit tearful even . .

We could respond to each other but we could not break through the
impasse to a critical encounter. I felt I had pushed this phase of our
relationship to its limit. I decided a change of pace might be of some
help. We began to meet twice a week rather than daily.

His behavior in the hospital changed dramatically during the next
month. He had intercourse with a female patient. He broke windows
in the nurse's dormitory with his fists. He smashed furniture in his
sister's home during a Christmas leave. He got into violent fights on

the ward. He ran off from the hospital and had to be brought back forcibly, etc. Still none of this behavior altered his intrapsychic structure. He would describe these events to me with complete emotional indifference. Nothing could involve him even in his own lived experience. He stated the problem succinctly: "Nothing . . nothing . . gets through."

His behavior gradually leveled off and he was put on a special milieu program. They discovered after a month that he was "really sick!" They even seemed surprised and somewhat bitter about it. They eliminated him from the program. They explained their decision to his sister on her next visit. I knew she was very close to her brother and deeply concerned about him. I wanted to assure her that any change in hospital policy would not affect my relationship with the client. So did I understand that she was a very mature young woman. I felt the client might soften in a relationship with two people devoted to his well-being. It did not happen as I expected. Still it did happen. The critical breakthrough erupted during our meeting together. It was the forty-third interview, the fourth month of therapy, and his sister was present:

> C. Oh, hell . . this is ridiculous . . all I need is a job . . I don't know all this stuff you're talking about . .
> S. Remember when you were home that time, and we were talking . . you said that, all of a sudden, things were coming to you . . you started coming out of it . . you started talking about things like responsibility . . you really started getting at the heart of this whole thing . .
> C. And that's what I want now . . I want to go for a visit . . I don't see . . that's not so wrong . .
> S. It's not wrong, but it just can't be arranged now . .
> C. It's not wrong . . except that I don't get to go for a visit . . that's what's wrong . . you just get me pissed-off and it doesn't do any good . .
> S. Well, now see, Johnny . . let me tell you this . . because you can't go home for a visit, you're getting all angry now . . this is the way you acted before when you were home . .
> C. (Loud and agitated) . . Damn well . . I got good reason to be mad . .
> S. Yes . . but don't you see . . I can't have you home with me like this . .
> C. I'm not going to be this way if you let me go for a visit . .

S. You can't guarantee that . . if you act this way here, then you certainly . .

C. Well, am I supposed to be happy that I don't get a leave? . . don't you understand that? . .

S. Don't you understand? . . right now you're . .

C. Now you wait . . listen to me . . don't you think I should be mad? . .

S. Maybe you should be upset . . but certainly you shouldn't act the way you're acting . .

C. I'm upset . . damn it, what the hell else . .

S. You should be able to say, "It's too bad, but maybe some other weekend" . .

C. Yeah . . it's just too bad . . shit . .

T. John . . there are so much bigger things at stake . . and yet you're focusing on this one weekend as if it were your whole life . . it isn't your life . .

C. It is to me . . this hospital isn't my life . .

T. It is right now . .

C. No it isn't . . all I need to do is get a job . . I have nothing to do with this hospital . .

T. Well, you can't be reached today . . I'm sure of that . . (smile) . .

C. *You* can't be reached today . .

T. We can't be reached either . . (smile) . . we're at an impasse . . a disagreement . .

C. Well I should think so . . I think that's pretty easy to figure out . . bullshit . .

T. Let's walk your sister back to her car and let her go on her way back to her family . . (C. and T. stand up) . .

C. So I don't get to leave . .

T. No . . not as far as I know . .

C. Well, you're the only one that can give me a leave . .

T. Now they said this just to shift the buck . .

C. They didn't shift the buck 'cause I'm not on their program now . .

T. The ward physician would have to give you a leave . . you know that . . but if they shifted the buck . . I'll accept it . . I'm convinced that nothing positive could come from a leave at this time . .

C. The ward doctor . . I wonder if he's there now . .

T. I don't know . . but I'm sure he's not just going to say, "Go ahead and go" . .

C. I don't know what you've got in your brain, but I want to leave and I'm going to ask him . .

T. Well, you can . . I'm just saying that I'm not going to do anything . .

S. John . . I have to go right now . .

T. Won't you walk with us to the car, John? . .

C. Well, can't she wait? . .

S. No . . I can't . . I mean it's settled, John . . you can't come home this weekend . . please accept that . .

C. (Loud and agitated) . . Well, maybe I don't want to accept that because it was promised to me . .

S. You said you realized I didn't promise . . (plaintive) . . I didn't promise you this weekend . .

C. Oh shit, man . . you're talkin' a bunch of nonsense . . (loud and violent) . . YOU DON'T GIVE A GOD DAMN FUCKIN' (in sudden rage strikes T. heavy blows to chest and face knocking him across the room and down) . . GOD DAMN, YOU GET ME PISSED-OFF FOR NO DAMN REASON AT ALL . . (tense traumatic silence) . .

T. (Looking directly at C. and getting slowly up from the floor) . . I know, John . .

C. (Still loud and agitated) . . Oh, look at you . . get up . . you're ridiculous . . it was promised to me to get a leave . . you know that was promised to me . . (C. sits back down in chair, head hung low) . . (T. slowly walks over, sits down in front of him) . . (traumatic silence again) . . (T., bleeding from nose and mouth, leans forward close to C.) . . (C. looks up at T. and continues, his voice broken by tears) . . I don't know what's the matter with me . . I want to be loved so God damn bad and nobody loves me for shit . .

T. (Tearful) . . (reaches over, touches C. gently on shoulder) . . I know, John . .

C. (Voice broken by strain and tears) . . You don't give a shit for nothin' . . (ruptures into turbulent sobbing) . . (voice mingled with explosive sobs) . . I don't feel it . . that's the trouble . . I don't feel love . . I don't know what love is . . I don't want to hurt you . . I don't know how I got that way . . (T. weeps) . . oh, don't cry . . shit . . I like Negro people . . I don't give a shit about nobody . . white people don't give a shit for nothin' . . Negro people are spiritual . . they love God . . but who the hell do you love . . all you like to do is just kill people . . you like to hurt them . .

S. (Soft and gentle) . . I don't like to hurt anybody . .

C. (Still strained and tearful) . . Oh shit . . I blame
this whole God damn thing on Americans . . all they
care about is conniving with people . . I was in India
and I was happy with religious people . . then something happened and now I'm back here . . and I just
don't belong here . . it causes me too much trouble with
everybody . . I just don't fit here . . and everything
is wrong . . and I can't change it . . (pause) . . listen
I just want a job so I can work . . I don't want to go
through all this crap . . I don't need that . . I need to
work . . to sweat a little . . to have someone to laugh
with while I'm working . . to have a family . . (out-
pour of sobbing again) . .

S. Of course you do, Johnny . .

C. (Tearful and angry) . . Well, why are you keeping
it from me? . . you sit here and you're crying for
some stupid reason . .

S. We're crying because we love you . .

C. Because you're afraid of me . . that's why . .

S. Because we're afraid of you? . .

C. Yes . . you're afraid of me . .

S. That isn't true . .

C. Oh, God damn bullshit . . you know you're afraid
of me . . that's why I can't go home with you . . I
can't even see my own God damn sister . . (weeps) . .

S. Johnny, I'm right here . .

C. (Tearful) . . Bullshit . . you're   not   here . . this
hospital is here . . that's what stands between you and
me . .

T. (Abrupt and resolute) . . But the hospital is where
you belong now, John . .

C. I can't . . I . . (starts to stand up) . .

T. (T. grips C. tightly by arm, pulling him back down
into his chair) . . Wait a minute . . this is where you
belong now . . because you're not well . .

C. (Pause) . . Having . . having . . having no direction . . and no freedom . . that's the thing I lack . .
there's no direction in this hospital . . I need . . I need
. . this is all wrong . . (pause) . .

T. What I'm feeling at this moment . . much more than
the hospital problem . . is all the hatred and violence
inside you . . that you can erupt . . and strike out . .
even at me . .

C. Oh, my God . . in other words you think I'd kill my sister . .

T. I don't know, John . . but I think you're just not well inside . .

C. (Pause) . . (soft) . . I don't know how I hit you . . (pause) . . I'm sorry I hit you . .

T. (Soft) . . I know . . I know you are . . (pause) . .

C. I feel cruel that I hit you . . I don't want to feel that way . . I want to . . (T. weeps from deep emotional pain) . . no . . I don't want that again . . (pause) . . you know what you're trying to do is *very hard* to do . . I had my love . . my . . my love for . . for every-thing . . my sister and everything . . cut out of me . . isn't that true, Dr. Johnson? . .

T. (Voice broken with sobs) . . I don't know . . (heavy sobbing) . . the only kind of feeling you could show me was to do that . . (heavy sobbing) . .

C. No . . that isn't the feeling . . I . . I did that to you because I want to be let out . . I'm telling you from the bottom of my heart . . and I no longer want to bullshit you . . (C. stands and strokes T. on shoulder and arm comforting him) . . really, man, I'm sorry . . I feel all shitty and rank that I did that . . really I hope you don't feel too bad . . no kidding . . I feel like hell . . (T. continues to weep . . C. continues to comfort him) . .

The mood of trauma gradually subsided. We sat for a time in intimate silence. Then we walked his sister to her car. I drove the client back to his ward in my car. We talked about truth and love.

The next day was Friday and I did not go to work. This gave my face a few days to heal. The client and I planned to meet at our usual three o'clock time on Monday. Yet he was waiting when I arrived Monday. He said he could not stay away from me and had thought about me all weekend. He expressed a troubled pain over what he had done. So did he express the desire to confront his sickness. He stopped several times during the day and we talked whenever possible. He slept under a tree outside my window when we were not together. I would stop and talk briefly whenever I left or entered the building. No one knew of the incident between us, but he was being transferred to a locked ward the next day because of his general disruptive behavior. He was waiting again that next morning and I went with him while he picked up his few meager belongings. Then we walked quietly to the locked ward. We had gone as far together as we could. The next step was for him alone. He knew it well:

"I need only the walls now." We said goodbye. I unlocked the door and watched him disappear down the dark corridor. We both knew this ordeal would be a new beginning or a further slip toward his psychic death. I will rejoice should he survive the crisis. I will weep should he flounder. Yet I am prepared even for that. I know what I will do. It is simple. I will begin again. I will not leave him to die.

Summary Reaction (Relationships I and II)

These were two examples of "Encounter Therapy" with severely distressed persons. Relationships developed because I responded only to the subjective interaction between us. I rejected everything else. I rejected social sciences, intellectual systems, cultural conventions. I rejected every organized conceptual structure which keeps man from himself—and from communion with other men. I responded only to the "now" of the subjective reality between us. The modes of congruent participation are responsive to such experiential immediacy. Their patterns vary with the unique expression of each client. Yet these varied modes and patterns emerge from but one primary source. They emerge from the therapist's subjective commitment to himself and to the client. This is not a commitment validated by science and buttressed by logical argument. It is rather a commitment forged from a process of subjective encounter with oneself and with other men. I seek both discovery and validation only in these subjective processes. My commitment is to the study of existence itself.

Subsequent Reaction (Relationship II)

The young man did survive the crisis and was discharged from the hospital a few months later. He told me as we parted: "Remember, you did me a whole lot of good!" I have tried to describe my subsequent reaction to the critical encounter with him: I wanted to discover boundaries for psychotherapy during the initial phase of my work. I wanted to discover terminal limits for the therapeutic experience. I felt intrinsic limits would emerge where personalities and relationships had no formal structure. I began work on the back wards of a large state hospital. I worked with anyone who showed signs of life and with many who showed none. A pattern of boundaries did emerge. Specific relationships were the guideposts for these boundaries. The outline was clear but there was no definitive closure. I could not reach the hypothetical turning point. I needed a relationship commitment which would convince me that I had gone as far as possible.

The significant patient in this struggle for closure was a seriously troubled young man. He had been in the hospital six months when we met. He had recovered from his initial disorganization and was now rational and coherent. His outward appearance was that of a typical and successful young adult. Yet, inwardly, he had been out of step with the world around him as long as he could remember. He described imaginative experiences from childhood which seem to have been preludes to his current religious and mystical confusion. He shared this current confusion with me: "See . . I'm a very holy person . . and divine . . I believe I'm like Jesus Christ . . I mean . . I believed that . . (heavy sigh) . . I don't know (pause) . . I believed that I'm . . I was the second coming of Christ . . and that I was pure and good until my heart was broken." So did he share with me other aspects of his confused identity: "Then I went and surrendered to a woman . . and when I got a piece of ass from her, that's when my soul changed to hers . . and I became like her in body and form and thinking and everything . . and now I feel that I am a woman . . and that's why I feel homosexual . . like with you . . I don't feel right toward you . . (pause) . . and that is the pool of blood that exists within me" (this composite of his confused identity was condensed from the full series of recorded excerpts).

We worked through these varied fears and established a significant rapport. Still we could not break through the interpersonal barrier between us. Then, toward the end of the fourth month, he wanted me to arrange a weekend leave for him. He had been violent and disruptive on the ward. So had he broken furniture, smashed windows, threatened his family, etc., on his last home visit. I told him I could not in all honesty recommend it. In a sudden rage he struck heavy blows to my chest and face. Then he sat down in his chair with his head hung low. I got up slowly from the floor and sat down close to him. My eyes were flooded with tears. He looked up at me. I touched him gently on the shoulder. We discovered each other in that brief moment. He broke into convulsive sobbing. Then my own emotional pain overwhelmed me. I sobbed openly with him. We intermittently cried and comforted each other until the mood of trauma gradually subsided. The pain we experienced together broke the interpersonal barrier. We shared the venture of a therapeutic relationship.

The intensity of that encounter gave me the definitive closure that I had been seeking. The hypothetical turning point was now a concrete reality. I knew for myself the limits and boundaries of psychotherapy. Other relationships would be different, but this would be the prototype for them. I had set the cornerstone for the foundation of my work.

Part III

Directions

Chapter 8
The End of Professionalism

I reject any organized pretense to an objective knowledge of man. I know only what I forge from my own personal struggle to live. I recognize only that subjective source of knowledge in other men. So must every therapist commit himself to subjective existence. So must every therapist rely on himself as a subjective person. One therapist does not express his subjective reactions to a client because "the data argue against it." Another does not express his body in therapy because "professional boundaries must be maintained." The sciences and the professions know nothing of subjective man. Each therapist must respond to his deepest subjective self. So too does such personal involvement by the therapist seem necessary to those in need of a therapeutic relationship:

> C. Have you looked at my records? . .
> T. No, I haven't . .
> C. Aren't you going to? . .
> T. I guess I don't care what others say about you, but only what I feel about you here . .
> C. Don't tell me I've finally met someone who really wants to know me! . .
> T. I guess maybe you have . . (pause) . .
> C. You know you're the first doctor I have talked to who would answer my questions . . the other doctors, they just ask questions, but they don't bother answering you . .
> T. They want you to be personal with them, but what they think is like . . none of your business . . (pause) . .
> C. You know I still find it hard to talk because I still think of you as a doctor . . .
> T. I know . . I forgot way back, but it may take you a little while . .

It was because she did forget that therapy began:

> C. You have soft eyes not like the hard eyes of the other doctors . . your eyes are warm . .
> T. I hope they speak from a warm heart . .
> C. I don't think of you as a doctor now . . you seem . . (pause) . .
> T. I know . . neither do I . .

She was nineteen years old and had just recovered from a prolonged period of extreme emotional disorganization when we met.
She was in control of her pathology now and wanted to make sure
she stayed that way. Yet during the third interview she softened
even as she discussed her constricted emotional control:

C. Right now I feel kinda stone . . kinda like stone . .

T. You feel sort of tight and stiff . .

C. Yeah, like I'm too reasonable now . .

T. You're just too sensible . .

C. (Laughs) Yeah, too sensible is the word.

T. (Laughs) You're so darn sensible about everything
now . . the logical you . . I don't know the emotional
you yet . .

C. But I talked about my problems and I never could
before . . I got them all out . .

T. But I guess it kinda felt to me like from a machine
. . not from the warm emotional you (C. and T.
laugh) . .

C. Like you turn me on . .

T. And it comes out like a ticker tape . . (pause) . .

C. If I had talked to you before, you couldn't have
understood me . .

T. I feel I wish I had known you then . . you had to
come back all by yourself and that works too . . but
you don't seem as whole as you might want to be . .

C. I know . . I don't think I want to stay like this . .
(pause) . . you mean you want to know all my emotions? . . not just part of me . . you want to know all my
different emotions? . .

T. You seem much more to me than I have known of
you . . you talked about your emotional problems but
it didn't seem to me as if you felt them here . .

C. I don't know how to do it . .

T. I guess I feel like . . (pause) . . like you talk about
tears but you don't cry . .

C. Uh huh . . I'd like to cry sometimes . . lots of
times I think I'm going to cry . . then I don't . .
(pause) . . what would you do if I just start crying? . .

T. Well, maybe you'll just have to see (C. and T.
laugh) . . I'm not going to give away any of my
secrets until you give away some of yours . . when
you share something of yourself with me, then I'll be
personal with you too (C. and T. laugh again) . .

She gradually became more personal and during the fifth interview
told of a bizarre and chaotic family background which culminated
at age fifteen in rape by her sister's husband, planned and abetted by
the sister herself. She learned to think of herself as an object "to be
used" and, after a sequence of sexual affairs, tried to take her own life.
She married a man from a similar background two years later and
the bizarre pattern has continued until the present hospitalization.
During the eighth interview she returned to the problem of her
emotional constriction:

C. I still feel stiff . .

T. Not quite like stone but still very stiff . .

C. Uh huh . . (pause) . . you know I think all my
life I've been sick . .

T. All your life you've really lived with inward confusion . .

C. I think it all started when I was real young and it just
took all these years to finally build up into what it
did . .

T. You had trouble all along, but then finally it just
exploded on you . .

C. Yeah . . you know one of the feelings I got when
I was sick was that a bomb was dropping and, just
before this bomb would explode, I felt everyone could
be whatever they wanted to be . . but I didn't want
to be anything else, yet I was afraid to stay the way I was
. . but I was afraid to change into something or someone else . . and there I was . .

T. You were just stuck there with no way to turn . .

C. Right . . and that's when it seemed like I was in
Hell . . just left in that one spot . . and I couldn't
get out . . I didn't know how to change . . I didn't
really know what I should do . . I was just completely
lost . . and I felt like there was no one to help me
either . .

T. A confused lonely Hell and no one to be with you
in any way . .

C. I still feel alone . . but it's not the kind of loneliness
I did have . .

T. It doesn't frighten you the same way . .

C. No, it doesn't frighten me now but I was real scared
. . I was scared of people around me . . I kept seeing
people in my past . .

T. You kept reliving relationships from the past . .

C. I'd look at a face and it would remind me of someone in my past . .

T. So you reacted to them as if they were that person . .

C. And I was kind of scared of them . . I remember
being scared of them and afraid . .

T. Uh huh . .

C. But when I was around each one longer, I got over
it . . being afraid of them . . I didn't feel anything
. . then I realized that they weren't people from my
past . .

T. I see . . as you got used to them you weren't afraid
of them . . and then gradually you realized that they
weren't even people from your past anyway . .

C. Right . . I'd see a woman who'd remind me of a
man I knew and at first I'd be afraid . . then a couple
days later I wasn't afraid . . then I'd realize it was a
woman not a man . .

T. Uh huh . .

C. And it was frightening at first . . I thought the bomb
had come and that I was livin' in another life . .

T. Uh huh . .

C. But it wasn't at all like the Heaven or Peace that was
promised . . it wasn't at all like that . .

T. You felt that you had died and . .

C. That I had gone to Hell . .

T. Yes . .

C. But that I had a chance to get out . .

T. And gradually you did get out . . the Hell slowly
cleared up for you . .

C. Yes . .

T. So you lived through death and Hell and then a
return from Hell . . back to yourself . . (pause) . .

C. I remember the matron at the jail . . she was real
stiff and her eyes were glassy . . she looked like a
zombi . . she frightened me . . that was just before
I got sick . .

T. She didn't seem real at all . .

C. No . .

T. And when you most needed someone warm and
soft there were only those hard unreal people about
you . .

C. You know what . . you might say I let fear overtake me . .

T. As if all your life you knew fear was after you . .

you always felt something was wrong . . and finally it
did overtake you . . and you lived for a while in deep
fear . . then . .

C. I fought it . . I overtook it . . I like to feel that
way . .

T. That you survived it and fear won't be the same
any more . .

C. Right . . now I can look to good things . . but I
want to remember the bad so I don't let it overtake me
again . . I can't just block it off . . I don't even want
to really . . I want to remember the bad so I won't let
the bad happen again . .

T. By letting in your whole life, rather than shutting any
of it out, then maybe you can move on to a new life . .

C. Yeah, because I sure don't want it to get in my way
again . . (pause) . .

T. You know, I think maybe I talk too much . .

C. You don't talk too much . .

T. I think that without all those words . . I think
maybe I did hear you down inside . . (pause) . .

C. I won't cry . .

T. That's something you won't let in . .

C. I'm not going to . .

T. You may let a lot of things into your life now . .
but not tears . .

C. When I'm alone I think it's best . . but I can't cry
even when I'm alone . . I don't know why, I just can't . .

T. You feel it would be best to cry alone and you might
let that in . .

C. If I could only cry when I'm alone . .

T. I see . . but when you are alone then you can't cry . .

C. I wonder why that is . . I haven't cried when I'm
alone . . when I'm alone, I just feel alone . . I don't
have any emotions . .

T. You don't feel anything unless you're in a relationship with someone . .

C. I feel that if I could cry . . have a real good cry . .
then I'd feel more human even . . I'd feel more softer
. . I know I'm not letting my feelings out as I should
. . I know there needs to be some way I can let my
emotions out and not be afraid . . there must be a way
. . I'll just have to wait and find it . .

T. How can you know the deeper emotional you and
not be afraid . .

C. Like part of me is still gone and I have to find that part . . and I think I can get a hold of it except I don't want to lose control over myself again . . I don't want to get too emotional . .

T. You feel that in trying to get back your other self you might get overwhelmed by emotion again . . that coming back together might be too much for you to control . .

C. Let's see if I can say it . . like this other self would be good for me, if I knew how to handle it . . if I didn't let it overtake this part of me . . if I could blend them . .

T. You so want to blend again with this deeper emotional part of yourself, but only on the condition that you remain in control . .

C. Right . .

T. You seem to say you know it would be a very serious risk and that . .

C. That I don't want to take it yet . .

T. Uh huh . . like one part of you has been kind of exiled and you don't want it to return until you're sure you can handle it . .

C. I have to be sure before I can . . I think, in time, my mind will be stronger . . like my mind is still weak . . but my heart is still there and I don't want my heart to overtake my mind . . that's what I'm trying to say . .

T. Yes . . you were dominated by your heart and look what happened . .

C. Right . .

T. Now your mind is in control and you're not going to risk that control until you're pretty sure . . but you do want your heart back too . .

C. Yes . . I want to put my whole heart into the things I do . .

T. But only when you're sure you still control what you do . .

C. I feel pretty good sayin' what I did 'cause that answered it . .

T. It gave you a clear picture of what you feel . .

C. Like when I came in here . . I remember going around to all the people . . I was real close to them . . I could understand them . . I went from one to another and each one I could understand . . but now these people here . .

T. These terrible people! . .

C. They're too much for me (C. and T. laugh) . .

T. You were all heart when you came here . .

C. Now I'm afraid I'll go insane if I pay attention to them . .

T. But now that your mind is in control . .

C. I just can't handle them . .

T. And I guess we're both a little amused by the extreme shift from the deepest compassion for these people to . . like the part of your heart that's exiled, so too must you exile these people . .

C. Yes . .

T. And though I agree with you about control of yourself . . still I would hate to see you shut your deepest emotions out from yourself . . and from others . . because I think there's something in me that feels very close to the girl who suffered so with the other patients . . (pause) . .

C. It's no good to be divided in two parts . . you should be just one person . .

T. I guess that's my feeling too . . there are parts of you that sound so human . . I guess I would like to see you take them back too . . (pause) . .

C. I saw a sad movie last night . . it was sad . . I forgot about that . . I did have a few tears . .

T. So even now you can be moved to tears by some things . .

C. I feel like I'd like to cry, but I don't want to cry because I'm sad . . I just want to cry to feel human . .

T. Uh huh . . you don't want just sad tears, but tears that will bring you back to yourself . .

C. I want it to be soft . . I want to be comforted . .

T. You don't want to cry alone . .

C. Maybe what I want is tears of joy just being myself again . .

T. Uh huh . .

C. I think when I finally realize that I am myself . . that I like myself . . then I think I may cry . .

T. Like tears of a deep reunion . .

In the twelfth interview she told me of crying alone on the ward and talked again of the personal nature of our relationship:

C. I don't know why I feel so close to you . . I do . . I like you . . it's the first time I ever told one person everything . .

T. You know, I feel too that in a very personal way we are close to each other . . yet I guess I want to know you even better . . I guess I feel . . I wish we could know all of you here . . (pause) . .

C. I cried a long time last night . . I don't know how long, but I cried until I went to sleep . . when I woke up, the door was locked and I thought the nurses had forgotten me . . I didn't want them to have forgotten me . . just locked me in there, you know . . so I yelled out to them . . and here they come and they had saved my tray . . it made me feel pretty good after I cried, and then knowing they hadn't forgotten me too . .

T. Uh huh . . so maybe no one was with you while you cried, but they hadn't forgotten you while you were crying . .

C. Right . .

T. So you felt the sadness inside and you had a deep cry by yourself . .

C. Like when I'm with you I talk about my sadness, but I don't feel quite so sad as I would by myself because I know you're here listening to me . .

T. Uh huh . . someone with you sort of keeps you from the loneliness that makes you cry . .

C. Right . . like I can talk to people, but they don't seem to understand it . . I feel like you understand . . not as a doctor, but as a human being . .

T. Uh huh . .

C. I think with any other doctor I don't feel personal at all . . it doesn't help me at all . .

T. So when you talk to some people . . even those who should understand . . it's just not heard at all . .

C. I tell you what most doctors do . . most doctors act like they're real superior . . but you . . you make me feel superior . . not big or anything . . but you make me feel like a human being . . you make me feel . . I don't know . .

T. Uh huh . . maybe you sense that . . that I really do feel that way about you and about myself . . that we are just two people struggling to find a way for ourselves and for others . . and that's all . .

The next interview she did cry in the relationship, but checked her tears before the hoped-for emotional reunion with herself. Yet she was one step closer:

C. I feel that, no matter how hard I try, my husband still doesn't understand how I feel . .

T. Uh huh . .

C. I can tell him about it and he can say he understands, but I can't help but feel a wall between us . .

T. You can't really feel he does understand . .

C. Even if we trust each other with our deepest, darkest secrets . . there's still something wrong . .

T. Uh huh . .

C. Like I told him they found that I couldn't have children, and he says, "Don't worry about it" . . I can't help but worry about it . . I always loved children, as long as I can remember I always loved children . . and no matter how much I talk to you or talk to myself I still can't convince myself . . (voice broken by tears) . . that I can make a life with my husband without children . . (pause) . .

T. Not only must you worry about not having children for yourself . . because you don't know if you can live without children . . but you don't know if your relationship with him can survive without children either . . (pause) . .

C. Almost as if . . (voice broken by tears) . . like if I knew I could never have children then I couldn't find anything really worth living for . . 'cause anybody else's children could never take the place of having my own children . . (tears) . . (pause) . . I think this is what really disturbs me . .

T. You feel if you can't get fulfillment of the love you need from a child of your own . . out of your own body . . then maybe it's just not worth going on . .

C. My relationship with my husband just won't be complete unless I have his child . . like I don't want children unless I can have his . .

T. You want a child out of your own body and you want it to be by him . . (long pause) . .

C. I think really I could feel close to just about any kind of a child . . you know, a child of any nationality . . as long as it's a child, I could love it and care for it . . but him . . I know by the past he doesn't feel close to these children as I do . .

T. Maybe you could fulfill yourself in just your love for a child . .

C. But I know it couldn't work out with him . .

T. The other part wouldn't work out, because he wouldn't share in your love for that child . .

C. Right . . I've told him I could even love a little Negro . . you know take care of a little Negro baby . . and he looked at me real funny and says, "Could you?" . .

T. I see . .

C. He just couldn't understand that . .

T. So when you say these things they just don't get through at all . . (pause) . .

C. This is why I think I've asked him for a divorce two times . . I think this is at the bottom of it all . .

The climax of therapy was the client's deep emotional reunion with herself. It occurred in the sixteenth interview:

C. I guess I just don't know what it would be like to trust someone . . but I know it couldn't be forced to happen . .

T. You're not sure how it would feel . . but you know that it would have to just happen . . (pause) . .

C. Maybe it's like I feel with you . .

T. Maybe it's happened between us . . (long pause) . .

C. I know there's something ugly in my husband, but I don't like to face it . . (pause) . . he uses people, even his mother and me . .

T. Even those people closest to him . .

C. I don't want to really face it . . but I know it's true . . and I know he won't change . . I know we can't ever . . (deep sobbing begins) . .

T. It hurts so much to think of losing him . . (pause) . .

C. (Deep sobbing continues) . . I always hoped he would change . . I need a dream to live on . .

T. You lose him and a dream too . . (pause) . .

C. (Deep sobbing continues) . . I wish I was mixed-up like I was when I came here . .

T. Then you could dream and it didn't matter . .

C. Now I understand . . and I hate it . . I want to stay like I was . . I won't give him up . . I'd rather stay sick all my life . .

T. You just can't live without that dream . .

C. I'll die without some hope . . I can't give him up . . (walks around room, still sobbing deeply) . . now I feel like smashing something . . good I'm not on the

ward or I would . .
T. I don't value property . .
C. I might smash that recorder . . I might smash you
too . . give you a black eye . .
T. It would go away . .
C. But it would hurt . .
T. I wouldn't mind . . (pause) . .
C. (Sits down as sobbing gradually subsides) . . I don't
know where I'd turn . . (pause) . . but there must be
some way for me . .
T. Maybe you could find another hope and another
dream . . (long pause) . . I have to leave now but you
might want to just stay here until you feel ready to return
to the ward . . remember I arranged it so you could
reach me should you want to talk . . (I kissed her gently on the cheek and left the room. I found two words
on a small piece of paper when I returned: "Thank
you.") . .

She was discharged from the hospital two weeks later. We arranged
for follow-up visits. She described the process of therapy herself: "I
felt all my emotions here . . I laughed . . I was angry . . I was
sad . . most of all, I cried . . now I feel like I can handle all of myself . . (pause) . . I know there will be bad times . . but I think
I can make it."

She had experienced an emotional communion with herself and
with another. I consider these subjective phenomena the primary
dimensions of psychotherapy. They must be investigated free from
the professional biases of medicine and psychology. They must be
comprehended in their own right. They must evolve their own experiential style and methodology.

Psychotherapy is not a professional routine. It is a personal venture.
The client is "like me." I reject any professional boundary between us.
Constructive change does not occur because of induced transference
but, conversely, because the client recognizes that "this is a *person*
and this person cares for me." I make it as just such a person in the
life of the client, or I fail.

The elimination of stereotypes does entail a risk. One must then
deal with the experiential phenomena themselves. Elimination of
the professional stereotype may alienate some clients. A female
client expected a stereotyped relationship with me. I did not "look or
act like a professional." She expressed her resentment: "You could be
just another jerk to me." Yet even that expression was the occasion
for an encounter between us. She entered into a personal interaction

with me. The interaction reached a climax and I held out my hand. She took it in both her own, trembled, and cried. She told me later, "had you been like I expected . . (pause) . . you never would have known I tremble."

I consider the professional stereotype a distorted facade that keeps both client and therapist from their deepest selves. The personal abstinence inherent in all professionalism is abhorrent to me. I participate in therapy on but one subjective premise. I participate on the personal knowledge that what has happened to each client could happen to me. I recognize only the reality of that subjective discovery.

The Existential Ground

on interpersonal existence

Camus: The Rebel

There is, in fact, nothing in common between a master and a slave; it is impossible to speak and communicate with a person who has been reduced to servitude. Instead of the implicit and untrammeled dialogue through which we come to recognize our similarity and consecrate our destiny, servitude gives sway to the most terrible of silences. If injustice is bad for the rebel, it is not because it contradicts an external idea of justice but because it perpetuates the silent hostility that separates the oppressor from the oppressed. It kills the small part of existence that can be realized on this earth through the mutual understanding of men. In the same way, since the man who lies shuts himself off from other men, falsehood is therefore proscribed and, on a slightly lower level, murder and violence, which impose definitive silence. The mutual understanding and communication discovered by rebellion can survive only in the free exchange of conversation. Every ambiguity, every misunderstanding, leads to death; clear language and simple words are the only salvation from this death. (It is worth noting that the language peculiar to totalitarian doctrines is always a scholastic or administrative language.)

Berdyaev: Solitude and Society

But the "I" is not content with communication with other "I"s in society and the state, in social institutions, communication by means of conditioned signs: it strives for communion with other "I"s, for entrance into genuine existence. All conditional communication relates to the world of objectivization, it is communication with objects. But the bursting-out toward communion is movement beyond objectivization toward true existence. The symbolization of communication is linked with varying degrees of objectivization. Communion predicates mutuality: one-sided communion is impossible. Unrequited love is not communion. In communion not only "I" is active, but "thou," as well. Only symbolic communication is possible with an object, and this does not have to be a mutual affair. Communion is possible only with an "I" who is "thou" for me, and this demands mutuality, i.e. the activity of "thou." Communion is possible only on the plane of existence, not on that of objectivization.

Buber: Between Man and Man

It would be wrong to identify what is meant here with the familiar but not very significant term, "empathy." Empathy means, if anything, to glide with one's own feeling into the dynamic structure of an object, a pillar or a crystal or the branch of a tree, or even of an animal or a man, and as it were to trace it from within, understanding the formation and motoriality of the object with the perceptions of one's own muscles; it means to "transpose" oneself over there and in there. Thus it means the absorption in pure aestheticism of the reality in which one participates. Inclusion is the opposite of this. It is the extension of one's own concreteness, the fulfilment of the actual situation of life, the complete presence of the reality in which one participates . . . this one person, without forfeiting anything of the felt reality of his activity, at the same time lives through the common event from the standpoint of the other.

on humanistic psychology

Kierkegaard: The Concept of Dread

It is not my purpose to write a learned work or to waste time looking up literary proof texts. Oftentimes the examples adduced in books on psychology lack the proper psychological-poetic authority. They stand there as isolated facts notarially attested, but precisely for this reason one does not know whether to laugh or weep at the attempt of such a lonely stickler to form some sort of a general rule. A man who with any degree of seriousness has concerned himself with psychology and psychological observations has acquired a general human pliability which makes him capable of being able to construct his example at once, one which, even though it has not authorization of the factual sort, has nevertheless a different kind of authority. As the psychological observer ought to be more agile than the tightrope dancer in order to be able to insinuate himself under the skin of other people and to imitate their attitudes, as his silence in confidential moments ought to be seductive and voluptuous in order that the hidden thing may find pleasure in slipping out and chatting quietly with itself in this fictitious inattention and quiet, so he ought also to have a poetical primitiveness in his soul to be able to create at once the totality of the rule out of that which in the individual is always present only partially and irregularly. Then when he has perfected himself he will not need to fetch his examples from literary repertoires and warmed-over, half-dead reminiscences but draws his observations directly and freshly from the water, still flopping and displaying the play of their colors. Neither will he need to run himself to death in order to make note of something. On the contrary, he will sit calmly in his chamber, like a detective who knows nevertheless everything that is going on. What he needs he is able to fashion at once; what he needs he has straightway at hand by virtue of his general practice, just as in a well-ordered house one does not need to go down to the street to fetch water but has it on his floor by high pressure. If he were to become doubtful, he is then so well oriented in human life and his glance is so inquisitorially sharp that he knows where he should seek and easily discover some individual or another who would be serviceable for his experiment. His observation will be as trustworthy as that of any other man, even though he does not support it with erudite quotations—for example, that in Saxony there was a peasant girl whom a physician had under observation, that in Rome there was an emperor of whom a historian relates, etc.—as though it were true that such things emerged only once every thousand years. What interest has it then for psychology? No, it is everywhere, occurs every day, if only an observer is there. His observation will have the stamp of freedom and the interest of reality, if he is prudent enough to verify it. To this end he imitates in his own person every mood, every psychic state, which he discovers in another. Thereupon he sees if he cannot delude the other by his imitation, whether he can draw him into the further development which is his own creation by virtue of the idea. Thus if one would observe a passion, one has to choose one's individual. Then the thing is to be quiet, silent, unobtrusive, so that one may lure the secret from him. Thereupon one practices what one has learned until one is able to deceive him. Thereupon one poetizes the passion and appears before him in passion's preternatural size. If this is done correctly, the individual will feel an indescribable relief and satisfaction, as does a demented man when one has found and poetically comprehended his fixed idea and then develops it further. If this does succeed, the failure may be due to a fault in the operation, but it may also be due to the fact that the individual was a poor example.

Chapter 9
The Validation
of Experience

I know my hand is mine because I open and close my fist at will. It is the exercise of that intentional movement that makes it mine. I want to grasp the mineness of my own being the way I grasp the mineness of my own hand. Science knows nothing of such mineness. It demands that I abandon my own being. It demands that I recognize "objective data" beyond my own subjective experience. I must refuse. I know something from direct encounter with it, or know it not at all. A journal editor returns a paper because "you offer no data to support your assumptions." I sent him the experience itself, but that was not enough. A rigged gimmick would have made all the difference. I refuse once more. The validity of my work must be judged by direct encounter with it. I will play no games.

This is the critical problem for me—the conflict between science and subjective reality. Define these terms as you will. Manipulate them as you like. They cannot be reconciled. Subjective experience cannot be reconciled with public validation. A subjective phenomenon can be validated only by a subjective encounter with it. Experiential phenomena *are* knowable, but only by direct subjective encounter. I know the phenomenon of empathy. I validate it each time I encounter it. Judges judging and raters rating validate nothing for me. I validate only what I encounter for myself. I know only what I make subjectively mine.

I do want to validate my work. I do want to critically assess it. Thus the experiential events which characterize the work must be made public. Still the process which validates these public events remains intrinsically a private one. Consequently, I will use only a methodology which involves my private being as directly as did the original experience. Validation becomes a sterile ritual which contributes nothing toward development of the work itself without such direct and personal involvement. The process of validation must be as subjectively vital as was the process of discovery. I reject any methodology which puts me experientially outside the investigated phenomena themselves.

Congruence, empathy, and positive regard have been reliably rated. I assert that the modes of congruence which I propose here could be

97

as easily distinguished. Congruent participation, modified congruent participation, and congruent body participation are unique and distinct phenomena. They could be reliably rated by judges.

Process changes in client behavior as a response to congruence, empathy, and positive regard have been reliably measured. They could be reliably measured as responses to the modes of therapy which I propose. The correlation of the proposed modes with progressive changes in client behavior would provide a validation acceptable to psychology. It would *not* be acceptable to me. I refuse once more. It would validate nothing for me since the ratings of others do not involve me. I reject any process of validation which does not directly involve the mineness of my own being. I can validate my work or the work of another only by direct encounter with it. I reject any methodology which is not personally and subjectively vital to me.

I do want a dialogue with others about the process of psychotherapy. I do want a critical interaction among therapists. Yet it must be a direct encounter with the other and with his work. I cannot encounter data about one's work. Only the therapist and his work itself are real to me.

I have tried to validate for myself the experiences presented here. I used a subjective methodology meaningful to me. I studied the modes of therapist intervention and their impact on the client, on me, and on the interaction between us. The introduction of a detached rater would contribute nothing to the process of validation. Each particular person must instead be his own judge. He must validate the phenomena himself by direct encounter with them. Only validation by direct encounter is useful validation. Any significant dialogue must be based on just such a direct method. Therefore, I want to present the work itself so that each reader can directly validate or directly reject it *for himself.* I recognize only such direct participation in the validation process. There is no way to avoid individual responsibility for the validation of subjective experience. Each one must ultimately be his own rater and his own judge.

I set two criteria for myself by which to validate the modes of therapist participation which I propose. Each mode must (1) be a unique and distinct phenomenon and (2) bring the client closer toward an experiential encounter with *himself* and with the *therapist.* I consider such *intra* and *inter*personal encounter the crux of personality change and development.

Empathic reflection is one of the five modes of therapy significant to me. I have found it a central mode in every pattern of relationship. It is well-documented and will not be a focus of further validation here. Nor will a further validation of metaphor communication be included since it is an ancillary mode of encounter. I want to concentrate at this point on the three primary modes of congruent participation.

Congruence is the cornerstone of therapy for me. It is congruence which makes empathy and positive regard authentic phenomena. I want only to discover alternate modes which can more directly express the phenomenon of congruence in the therapeutic relationship. I describe this general process as "congruent participation." So does congruent participation refer to one of the three *specific* modes of congruent expression. It is the introduction of the therapist's subjective reactions into his relationship with the client. It is for me a valid mode of therapy since it meets the two criteria which I have described. It is a unique and distinct phenomenon which can be clearly contrasted to any other therapy mode, e.g., to interpretive and direct intervention since congruent participation is an *expression* by the therapist *of his own* subjective experience rather than an interpretation by the therapist *of the client's* subjective experience. It is, for me, unique and distinct, but each one must make that decision for himself. Congruent participation also meets the second criterion of validation since it brings the client closer toward an experiential encounter with himself and with the therapist. Yet each reader must also decide that for himself. I can only make public the mode, the client response, and my own personal reaction. The rest is the private responsibility of each one alone.

These are specific examples of congruent participation taken from some of the work presented here. I have included page and line numbers so that the extracted mode can also be studied in its original context:

(Congruent participation in italics: Page 28, Line 04)

C. I was kind of wondering if one reason why it's harder for me to establish anything with you, and with most people probably, that aren't like me . . maybe that's why they're not kind of bums, screwed-up or wondering or anything . . maybe I feel that I can't trust them 'cause it'd be so much easier for them to reject me . . 'cause it'd be so easy for them to say, "Here's this guy who's all screwed-up so I won't have anything to do with him" . . people that I go around with are all screwed-up themselves so they can't really say, "He's a bum, he's wasting his life, I don't want anything to do with him" . . but people who aren't like this, they can do that, and I guess sometimes they do . . they don't want anything to do with me . . maybe I just don't work really all the way at establishing anything if I don't feel an immediate bond . . (pause) . .

T. *You don't . . you don't feel that . . that I know what it is . . to be fucked-up right . .*

C. Of course I know this . . but it's not a question of me sitting here saying to myself that I know that you know what it's like to be fucked-up and everything . . that has nothing to do with this . . what the hell . . so I know this . .

T. *You mean . . you don't feel that I as a person . .*

C. I feel it consciously . . but what about inside? . .

T. *You don't feel the fucked-up me inside yourself! . .*

C. No . . you're . . you know . . like with "Duke," he's all screwed-up, immediately I felt sort of a something between us . . you know with most people I don't 'cause they're not like that . . and oh, consciously I can say to myself that, you know, you can understand, et cetera, et cetera, et cetera . . but where is there anything between us! . .

T. I have to look at you as something different from me to understand . .

C. Maybe that's it . .

T. I can't feel with you the way he does . . (pause) . . *you don't . . you don't feel . . that part of me never really gets through to you . . all the unknown, ambiguous, dark corners in my life . . my past, my present, and possibly the future . . you don't sense those . .*

C. No, as a matter of fact I never have at all . . like with "Duke," we can talk about things . . like yesterday we sat down on the beach for awhile and we were both very tired because we didn't go to bed 'till about 6:30 in the morning yesterday either . . and we just sort of looked at each other and said, "How fucking ridiculous . . . we're wasting our lives doing absolutely nothing and all we can do is laugh about it" . . and finally I said, "Shit, this is ridiculous, we're all fucked-up and we know it, we don't even care enough to do anything more than laugh" . . we sat there and (laughs) "wow, wow, we're all fucked-up, look what we're doing" (laughs) . .

Comment: My congruent entry into the relationship initiated an interaction which culminated in a climactic encounter between us.

(Congruent participation in italics: Page 60, Line 06)

C. So then I started sleeping during the day and staying awake at night . .

T. You didn't want to have sex with your boy . .

C. And he didn't ever ask me to and I didn't ever ask
him to . .

T. You didn't want that out in the open . . that you
might want to have sex with each other . .

C. No . . definitely . . I am fixed up altogether different than I was fixed up on the outside . . I was
afraid of lightening shootin' in my house and I put on a
dress to go out and I took my son with me most of the
time and . .

T. *You know, I used to worry about having sex with
my mother* . .

C. You know, the Bible brings a lot of filth into people's
minds . .

T. It got you thinking about sex with your boy . .

C. (Emphatic) . . No it did not . . it was somebody
else's thought mirrored through my brain . . that was
their mind, not my mind . . I never once even thought
of it . .

T. *Well, in my mind I'm telling you I have . . I
thought of sex with my mother . . in my own mind
and nobody put it there . . I thought of it and it worried
me . . it worried me a lot* . .

C. Well, it sounds like I want to have sex with my father,
brother, or somethin', but I haven't . .

T. So these could be thoughts you have . . (the same
interaction sequence) . . it's possible to screw your
father, your brother, your son . . it's all possible . . *it's
possible for me to screw my mother . . if I had a
sister, I could screw her* . .

C. Well, my sister was in a girl's school and so she had
me feel her breasts and it disgusted me . .

T. I see, sometimes sex stuff gets mixed-up between girls
too . . it is possible for girls to have sex with girls . .
it's possible for men to have sex with men . . *I've
known a lot of queers . . even been close to some . .
but I said, "I'd rather fuck women"* . .

C. Yes, I know . . Judy stuck her finger up me one
time and I told her I preferred a man . .

T. I see . . you just clearly said: "Okay, so you can
finger-fuck me, but I'd rather have a man do it" . .
you made a decision . . you said: "I'd rather have a
man fuck me" . . these are just decisions everyone
has to make . .

Comment: My subjective participation in the relationship moved her closer toward an encounter with her own subjective experience. She began this sequence by rejection of her sexual preoccupation as "somebody else's thought mirrored through my brain" and ended with a coherent discussion of personal sexual experiences.

Modified congruent participation is for me another unique and distinct mode of therapy. It can be contrasted to interpretive and direct methods since it does not impose any interpretive structure on the phenomenal world of the client. It is rather a personal participation in the phenomenal world itself. It can be contrasted to interaction by the introduction of shared fantasy since nothing is "made-up" in any mode of congruent participation. The "pathology" of the client *is* his current real world and the therapist enters that world by utilization of his own "potential pathology." It is not interaction focused in imagined abstraction, but interaction concentrated in the experiential reality between client and therapist. It can also be contrasted to empathy since it is not a reflective response to the phenomenal world of the client but an active participation in it.

(Modified congruent participation: Page 30, Line 30)

T. But being queer and inadequate . . that has something to do with you right now . . it's harder to turn that away than something that happened in the past . .

C. But I don't like to be bothered by it either, so I don't bother with it very often . . I'm not queer . . of course not, why should I be . . so I can't make love (laughs) . . what a joke . .

(Climactic laughter by both C. and T.)

C. Fuck, Jesus Christ, what a fucking joke, well no man . .

T. You're an inadequate queer and so what . .

(More laughter)

C. That's not so funny really . .

T. I don't see why not . .

C. Well . .

T. What's wrong with . . I mean I really don't see, and I can get a little feeling of that, so what . . you're an inadequate queer, so what, I don't even care . .

C. (Laughs) That's horrible . . no, I should care . .

(Climactic laughter again by both C. and T.)

T. Who told you that? . .

C. No, shit, Jesus Christ, I like to . . I, you know, fuck . . I don't want to be a queer and I want to fuck . . but you know, if I can't, so what . .

T. (Intense laugh) . .

C. What a piece of shit that is . . if I can't feel something about that, for Christ' sake . . feel about fucking . . God, fucking's a weird word . . what a weird word . .

T. Fucking asshole strikes me as a weird word . . (laughs) . .

C. Yeah, but fucking . . what a sound, what a sound . . fuck . . how the hell did they ever invent fuck . . fuck you . .

T. (Laughs) It's a good word though . .

C. Really . . it's so feeling . .

T. We don't know which came first, the feeling or the word . . but the word is . . mother-fuckin' is another good word . .

C. But when I think of the word fuck . .

T. Mother-fuckin' . . I like mother-fuckin' too . .

C. Yeah . .

T. You don't like mother-fuckin'? . .

C. Yeah . .

T. You like mother-fuckin'! . .

C. I don't use it very often, I don't think, but it's . .

T. I even like cock-sucker too . . but I don't think you do (laughs) . .

C. Yeah, I do . .

T. Mother-fuckin' cock-sucker is a good one . .

C. Yeah, it is . .

T. You like it . .

C. Yeah, it's got such a sound . . such a filthy rotten sound to it . . it's so dirty . . when I think about making love to a girl, I don't really think about fucking . . fucking is an insult . . fucking is dirty, filthy rotten, and mean, and evil and everything . . fucking is taboo . . fucking is filthy, it's a filthy sound . . fuck . .

T. It even sounds, you know, the actual process is juicy and it could be fuck, fuck . .

C. Right . .

T. Juice, juice kind of thing . .

(Laughter once more by both C. and T.)

Comment: The client and I encountered each other in his bizarre experiential world. Such a modified congruent encounter serves as a bridge to direct congruent encounter.

(Modified congruent participation: Page 75, Line 07)
C. (Laughter) . . You better watch what you're doin'

. . you're goin' to start paintin' on the walls or somethin' . .

T. I know, and I really don't know if I can come back
. . I don't want to . . I don't want to come back to the
burden of you . .

C. Yeah . .

T. I just . . you know, I'd rather just sorta drift
around and just not have to be concerned about you . .

C. (Laughter) . . God damn psychologist playing with
the walls . . fuck . . what's the matter with you . .
someone see you doing that you're goin' to get fired . .

T. Oh, well . .

C. (Laughter) . . I've never seen you like this before . .

T. You haven't, huh? . .

C. God damn . . you're actin' human . .

T. Hmm . . yeah . . it's possible for me to be as
sorta crazy as you are if I wanta be . .

C. Yeah . .

T. And to be as unhappy about it too . . I'm not . .
I'm not . .

C. You don't seem too happy now . .

T. I'm not havin' a good time . .

C. You look like you're sufferin' through me . .

T. I'm unhappy . .

C. Or with me . .

T. And not . . not really frightened . . but a little bit
uneasy . . and . . and a little bit tearful even . .

Comment: We met on a new experiential level and the client
understood it: "You're sufferin' through me . . with me." The
modified congruent encounter was again a bridge to direct congruent
encounter.

Congruent body participation is one more unique and distinct mode
of therapy for me. It is contrast to body contact in direct therapy
since it is not a symbolic body relationship. The therapist is his own
congruent person rather than a symbolic figure. It is a *personal* body
encounter between the client and the therapist himself.

(Congruent body participation in italics: Page 54, Line 34)

C. (Tearful) . . I have too many faces . . too many
laughin' . . (pause) . . you cryin' for me too? . .

T. I'd like to cry with you . . (*I took one of her hands
in both of mine*) . .

C. (Sigh) . . You see, I got everything tuned in now

. . (pause) . . they say they oughta get six months in jail for that . . looks like that guy said he seen me with a priest on television . . (pause) . . what do you feel in this hand now? . . should I take off that ring? . . (I held her other hand) . .

T. No, that's all right . . this hand doesn't feel quite as warm . . (pause) . . now it does . . now it's beginning to feel warm . .

C. Some people see different things in them . . sometimes they see God or Jesus . .

T. I come closer to seeing you here than I have . . (pause) . .

C. Are you an atheist? . .

T. I believe in you . .

C. Why . . because you have to believe in yourself, huh? . .

T. I believe in myself and in you . . (pause) . .

C. You think you can bring me back to normal by that? . .

T. Sometimes believing in someone . .

Comment: The body contact emerged from my deepest congruent self in response to her tears. It was a bridge which sustained the significant interaction between us.

(Congruent body participation in italics: Page 62, Line 07)

C. Now you're really goin' to cuss me out when you play that back . . you'd like to slap my face now, wouldn't you? . .

T. *(I reached over slowly and touched her face gently with my hand)* . . That's all I want to do . . touch you gently . .

C. I get embarrassed . . that's why I laugh . .

T. I see . . it's easier sometimes to laugh . .

C. Like my girl friend, Judy . . she laughs when she's embarrassed . .

T. Yes, there's a kind of embarrassed laughter . . people giggle sometimes under tension . . (pause) . . I guess it would be less embarrassing if someone did slap you rather than just touch you gently . .

C. I better go back to the ward now, huh? . .

T. You think it's time to go? . .

C. Don't you? (laughs) . .

T. It probably is about time, but otherwise I'd like to talk to you for a long while yet . . (pause) . .

C. What kind of a mind you got anyway? (laughs) . .

T. Almost as funny as yours, I guess . .

Comment: Her response to my congruent body participation was relevant, intimate, and very sensitive. She moved closer toward authentic awareness and appropriate expression of her own emotional experience.

I have tried to present specific examples of the three primary modes of congruent participation and the specific reaction to each mode. I have taken these modes out of the interaction patterns in which they originally occurred. I now want to present some combinations of modes in emergent interaction with one another.

(Congruent participation in combination with empathic reflection; Congruent participation in italics: Page 89, Line 13)

T. *And though I agree with you about control of your-self . . still I would hate to see you shut your deepest emotions out from yourself . . and from others . . be-cause I think there's something in me that feels very close to the girl who suffered so with the other patients . . (pause)* . .

C. It's no good to be divided in two parts . . you should be just one person . .

T. *I guess that's my feelings too . . there are parts of you that sound so human . . I guess I would like to see you take them back too . . (pause)* . .

C. I saw a sad movie last night . . it was sad . . I forgot about that . . I did have a few tears . .

T. So even now you can be moved to tears by some things . .

C. I feel like I'd like to cry, but I don't want to cry because I'm sad . . I just want to cry to feel human . .

T. Uh huh . . you don't want just sad tears, but tears that will bring you back to yourself . .

C. I want it to be soft . . I want to be comforted . .

T. You don't want to cry alone . .

C. Maybe what I want is tears of joy just being myself again . .

T. Uh huh . .

C. I think when I finally realize that I am myself . . that I like myself . . then I think I may cry . .

T. Like tears of a deep reunion . .

Comment: She seemed to discover the deeper significance of emotional experience by her participation in this combination of modes.

(Congruent participation in combination with congruent body participation;
Congruent participation in italics: Page 56, Line 11)

C. No . . I was fightin' with my husband . . and he was threatening my life . . runnin' through the house . . and I got mad at the police . . and the police was always comin' over there . . and . .

T. *Now look, Bonnie . .*

C. You want me to forget that, huh? . .

T. *No, I don't mind you talking like that . . I'm just sayin' it's tough as hell for me to sit here and talk with you and not really feel you here . .*

C. Oh you feel me here, I get a little thrill in my stomach and in my chest . . does that mean I'm afraid of you or I'm a whore? . . my trouble is I'm too hard-headed, huh? . . boy, they're clankin' now . .

T. (I stood up, held her face in my hands and looked into her eyes) . . I just want to touch you gently to let you know I'm here . .

C. (Voice tender and hushed) . . Sounded for a minute you thought my skin was meltin' and I looked horrible . .

T. No, you just feel soft and warm . .

Comment: She responded to this combination of modes by a sudden shift from disengaged incoherence to intimate and personal participation. It initiated the most prolonged and most significant series of interactions in the first phase of our relationship.

(Congruent participation in combination with empathic reflection;
Congruent participation in italics: Page 89, Line 42)

C. I don't know why I feel so close to you . . I do . . I like you . . it's the first time I ever told one person everything . .

T. *You know, I feel too that in a very personal way we are close to each other . . yet I guess I want to know you even better . . I guess I feel . . I wish we could know all of you here . . (pause) . .*

C. I cried a long time last night . . I don't know how long, but I cried until I went to sleep . . when I woke up, the door was locked and I thought the nurses had forgotten me . . I didn't want them to have forgotten me . . just locked me in there, you know . . so I yelled out to them . . and here they come and they had saved my tray . . it made me feel pretty good after I cried, and then knowing they hadn't forgotten me too . .

T. Uh huh . . so maybe no one was with you while

you cried, but they hadn't forgotten you while you were
crying . .
C. Right . .
T. So you felt the sadness inside and you had a deep
cry by yourself . .
C. Like when I'm with you I talk about my sadness,
but I don't feel quite so sad as I would by myself because I know you're here listening to me . .
T. Uh huh . . someone with you sort of keeps you from
the loneliness that makes you cry . .
C. Right . . like I can talk to people, but they don't
seem to understand it . . I feel like you understand
. . not as a doctor, but as a human being . .
T. Uh huh . .
C. I think with any other doctor I don't feel personal
at all . . it doesn't help me at all . .
T. So when you talk to some people . . even those
who should understand . . it's just not heard at all . .
C. I tell you what most doctors do . . most doctors act
like they're real superior . . but you . . you make me
feel superior . . not big or anything . . but you make
me feel like a human being . . you make me feel . . I
don't know . .
T. *Uh huh . . maybe you sense that . . that I really do
feel that way about you and about myself . . that we
are just two people struggling to find a way for ourselves and for others . . and that's all . .*

Comment: She seemed to deeply experience and clearly recognize
the interpersonal significance of my congruent participation in our
relationship. This combination of modes moved us closer to each
other and her closer to the climactic encounter with herself a few
interviews later.

These five modes of communication are the modes of therapy
important to me. Each relationship develops its own emergent pattern of these modes. The relationships analyzed in some detail here
represent four such distinct patterns. The relationship with the first
young man utilized empathy, congruent participation, and modified
congruent participation. The relationship with the more disturbed
young man required all five modes of participation. So were all five
modes of participation needed with the more disturbed female client.
The emergent pattern with the other young woman did not require
modified congruent participation because she was sufficiently engaged in the relationship to make direct congruent encounter

possible without a preliminary modified encounter.

I validate these emergent patterns by contrast of early and late segments from the overall relationship. It is the same method as was used to validate specific modes. I study the change in the client, in me, and in our relationship as a function of my intervention. The intervention here is the emergent pattern of congruent participation.

The change from early to late in the interaction with the first young man seems best characterized by the change in his reference to our relationship:

> (Early) C. No . . you're . . you know, like with "Duke," he's all screwed-up, immediately I felt sort of something between us . . you know with most people I don't, 'cause they're not like that . . and oh, consciously, I can say to myself that, you know, you can understand . . et cetera, et cetera, et cetera, but where is there anything between us! . . (Late) C. I guess if I'm with somebody that . . that won't hold it against me . . and who goes through it himself . . and understands, maybe not completely, but understands at least how I feel about it . . and understands that I do laugh at it . . somebody just as fucked-up as I am . . then I can drop the smile and the big laugh . . even then we can laugh at it but, by God, I realize I'm laughing at it and I can say, "Why the fuck am I laughing at it?" . . but even then it sometimes becomes too much words, too much saying, well, maybe it's this, maybe it's that, maybe I did this, maybe this happened . . but still it's a little closer than it is with anybody else, anytime . .

The change in the interaction with the more disturbed young man can also be seen by a similar transition in the nature of our relationship:

> (Early) C. You remind me of a human being (3rd hour) . . through C. Now you're actin' human (23rd hour) . . to the reality of a human response (Late) C. (Stands and strokes T. on shoulder and arm comforting him) . . Really, man, I'm sorry . . I feel all shitty and rank that I did that . . really, I hope you don't feel too bad . . no kidding . . I feel like hell (43rd hour).

The change in the interaction with the more disturbed of the two women can best be seen by the change in her perspective toward the hospital and toward her sickness itself:

> (Early) C. This is the funny farm isn't it? . . they're goin' to turn you into a bunch of little animals, aren't they? . . I can talk to anything looks like . . (giggling laughter) . .
> T. You can talk to anyone and anything . .
> C. But I don't know what they say though . .
> T. What they say back to you? . .
> C. Yeah . . who do you think you are, my mother? . . who do you think you are, my father? . . who do you think you are, my sister? . . who do you think you are, my brother? . . everybody's switched around up there, out there, in there . .

T. They keep switchin' . . that makes it tough . .

C. And I get crunchin' in my head like a stapler . . and there's telephones in my head . .

T. You have the whole works, don't you? . .

C. And things flyin' through my brain . . and I can feel aches and pains and . .

(Late) C. You wouldn't want to be locked up, would you? . .

T. I guess in my life there have been times . . when it might have seemed best for a while . .

C. Yeah . . is that why you went into psychiatry?

T. You're wondering if maybe I'm concerned about people who have troubles because I've had troubles myself . .

C. Everybody's got problems . . (pause) . . I'd just like to know what's going on inside my head . .

T. You would like to understand what it's all about a little better . .

The change in the interaction with the second young woman can best be seen by the change in her description of herself:

(Early) C. I feel that if I could cry . . have a real good cry . . then I'd feel more human even . . I'd feel more softer . . I know I'm not letting my feelings out as I should . . I know there needs to be some way I can let my emotions out and not be afraid . . there must be a way . . I'll just have to wait and find it . .

(Late) C. I felt all my emotions here . . I laughed . . I was angry . . I was sad . . most of all, I cried . . now I feel I can handle all of myself . . (pause) . . I know there will be bad times . . but I think I can make it . .

I validate my work and the work of others by such a study of scripts, tapes, and films. I validate it by direct encounter with the phenomena themselves. The events presented here were modes of subjective communion "between man and man." Such interpersonal processes must be studied along with intrapersonal processes such as commitment, autonomy, and congruence. These latter are processes of subjective communion "between man and himself." I consider these *inter* and *intra*personal processes crucial to the future development of man. They are not his "soft underbelly." They are the existential *guts* of man.

The focus for the experiential research which I propose is the subjective process of psychotherapy. The critical factor in the research method which I propose is the personal encounter by the investigator himself. It is only by such critical encounters with oneself, with others, and with subjective reality that these phenomena can be discovered and validated. It is only through a research focused on these phenomena that modern psychology can be redefined as the "study of existence."

The patterns of these experiential events will emerge only from subjective exploration. They will emerge only from direct dialogue between persons deeply immersed in these crucial subjective processes. I have tried to initiate such a dialogue here. I have not presented data about my work. I have tried to present the work itself. It may be valid to some of you. I know many of you will reject it and me. My subjective extremism will offend you. You will agree with those who wanted me eliminated from psychology. You will say, as many others have, "You go too far." I can only answer you as I have answered them—I seek to go further.

The Existential Ground

on systematic psychology

Sartre: The Emotions

If it is necessary that there be later a rigorous concept of "man" . . . this concept can be envisaged only as the crown of a finished science, that is, one which is done with forever. It would still be only a unifying hypothesis, invented to co-ordinate and grade the infinite collection of facts which have been brought to light. This is to say that the idea of man, if ever it takes on a positive meaning, will be only a conjecture aiming to establish connections between disparate materials and will attain verisimilitude only by its success. . . . Thus, the idea of man can be only the sum of the established facts which it allows us to unite. However, if some psychologist were to use a certain conception of man before this ultimate synthesis were possible, it would be a strictly personal act, a conducting wire as it were . . and their first duty would be never to lose sight of the fact that it was a regulating concept.

It follows from so many precautions that psychology, insofar as it claims to be a science, can furnish only a sum of miscellaneous facts, most of which have no connection with the others. What can be more different, for example, than the study of the stroboscopic illusion and the inferiority complex? This confusion is not due to chance but to the very principles of the science of psychology. To expect the *fact* is, by definition, to expect the isolated, to prefer, because of positivism, the accidental to the essential, the contingent to the necessary, disorder to order; it is, on principle, to cast what is essential into the future: "That will do for later, when we shall have assembled enough facts." In short, psychologists do not realize that it is just as impossible to get to essence by accumulating accidents as to reach 1 by adding figures to the right of 0.99.

If their aim is to accumulate details of knowledge there is nothing to be said; one simply does not see what interest there is in these labors of a collector. But if they were animated, in their modesty, by the hope, in itself praiseworthy, that later on, on the basis of their monographs, an anthropological synthesis will be realized, they are in full contradiction with themselves. It will be said that this is precisely the method and ambition of the natural sciences. The answer to that is that the natural sciences do not aim at knowing *the world,* but the possible conditions of certain general phenomena. This notion of *world* has long since vanished beneath the criticism of methodologists, and precisely because one could not both apply the methods of the positive sciences and hope that they would one day lead to discovering the meaning of the synthetic totality which one calls *world*. But *man* is a being of the same type as *the world*. . . . Psychology should resign itself to doing without human reality for precisely that reason.

Kierkegaard: Concluding Unscientific Postscript

Who is to write or complete such a system? Surely a human being; unless we propose again to begin using the strange mode of speech which assumes that a human being becomes speculative philosophy in the abstract, or becomes the identity of subject and object. So then, a human being—and surely a living human being, i.e. an existing individual. Or if the speculative thought which brings the systems to light is the joint effort of different thinkers: in what last concluding thought does this fellowship finally realize itself, how does it reach the light of day? Surely through some human being? And how are the individual participants related to the joint effort, what are the categories which mediate between the individual and world-process, and who is it again who strings them all together on the systematic thread? Is he a human being, then he is also an existing individual. Two ways, in general, are open for an existing individual: *Either* he can do his utmost to forget that he is an existing individual, by which he becomes a comic figure, since existence has the remarkable trait of compelling an existing individual to exist whether he wills it or not. . . . *Or* he can concentrate his entire energy upon the fact that he is an existing individual. It is from this side, in the first instance, that objection must be made to modern philosophy; not that it has a mistaken presupposition, but that it has a comical presupposition, occasioned by its having forgotten, in a sort of world-historical absentmindedness, what it means to be a human being. Not indeed, what it means to be a human being in general; for this is the sort of thing that one might even induce a speculative philosopher to agree to; but what it means that you and I and he are human beings, each one for himself.

on subjective validation

Kierkegaard: Concluding Unscientific Postscript

When subjectivity is the truth, the conceptual determination of the truth must include an expression for the antithesis to objectivity, a memento of the fork in the road where the way swings off; this expression will at the same time serve as an indication of the tension of the subjective inwardness. Here is such a definition of truth: An objective uncertainty held fast in an appropriation-process of the most passionate inwardness is the truth, the highest truth attainable for an existing individual. At the point where the way swings off (and where this is cannot be specified objectively, since it is a matter of subjectivity), there objective knowledge is placed in abeyance. Thus the subject merely has, objectively, the uncertainty; but it is this which precisely increases the tension of that infinite passion which constitutes his inwardness. The truth is precisely the venture which chooses an objective uncertainty with the passion of the infinite.

Kierkegaard: Concluding Unscientific Postscript

Objectively we consider only the matter at issue, subjectively we have regard to the subject and his subjectivity; and behold, precisely this subjectivity is the matter at issue. This must constantly be borne in mind, namely, that the subjective problem is not something about an objective issue, but is the subjectivity itself. For since the problem in question poses a decision, and since all decisiveness, as shown above, inheres in subjectivity, it is essential that every trace of an objective issue should be eliminated. If any such trace remains, it is at once a sign that the subject seeks to shirk something of the pain and crisis of the decision; that is, he seeks to make the problem to some degree objective. If the Introduction still awaits the appearance of another work before bringing the matter up for judgment, if the System still lacks a paragraph, if the speaker has still another argument up his sleeve, it follows that the decision is postponed. Hence we do not here raise the question of the truth . . . in the sense that when this has been determined, the subject is assumed ready and willing to accept it. No, the question is as to the mode of the subject's acceptance; and it must be regarded as an illusion rooted in the demoralization which remains ignorant of the subjective nature of the decision, or as an evasion springing from the disingenuousness which seeks to shirk the decision by an objective mode of approach, wherein there can in all eternity be no decision, to assume that the transition from something objective to the subjective acceptance is a direct transition, following upon the objective deliberation as a matter of course. On the contrary, the subjective acceptance is precisely the decisive factor.

Chapter 10
The Metaphysics
of Psychotherapy

I am a psychotherapist. I am neither a philosopher nor a theologian. Yet psychology and psychiatry have failed. They are dominated by reductive systems which destroy the existential reality of man. Such systems cannot encompass the critical events of human existence. I want to explore these critical events as I experience them in psychotherapy.

I must first define the pathology treated by psychotherapy. I use the term *pathology* because it connotes the disruption of a natural condition. The natural state of man exists when all his potential resources are available to him. A pathological condition exists when man has been estranged from the human potentials within him. The clients I meet in psychotherapy suffer from this pathology of self-estrangement.

I want to comment further on this pathology and its treatment. A young male client told me, "I am helpless because I am afraid." He could describe his fear, but he was too threatened to encounter it. The intellectual descriptions but compounded his estangement from the fear and from himself. Then an extra-therapy event precipitated an emotional crisis. He trembled now and the language was no longer intellectual:

> C. I'm queer . . I knew I was and then I let him suck me . .
> T. Someone sucked you off and that makes you queer . .
> C. Yeah . . I knew I was . . and now this . .
> T. You worried about it . . but now this makes it final . .

The client collapsed into a state of prolonged and convulsive sobbing. The emotional impact of the extra-therapy event had broken the intellectual facade. This was the therapeutic climax of that breakthrough. It thrust him into the pain of an existential encounter.

I want to explore the dynamics of this concrete moment in psychotherapy. It will serve as a prototype for any critical encounter which can generate personality change. The significance of the encounter

115

must be understood in relation to the client's dilemma: "I am helpless because I am afraid." His own words are a succinct statement of the problem. He is helpless because his reaction to fear has estranged him from himself. He constricted his emotional being to isolate the sexual threat. He transformed the experience of fear into an intellectual construct. The act which transformed the existential threat into a logical construct transformed the self into a logical operation at the same time. The reactions we make to the lived world determine, in turn, the structure of the self which confronts that world. The emotional constriction was the pathological reaction which the client made to fear. The constriction destroyed the potency of the threat, but at the same time destroyed the potency of the self. It reduced the fear, but so did it cripple the self with its innate potentials. One of these innate potentials is the capacity of the self to choose and will its own destiny. The client was "helpless" because the act which reduced the fear made his will an intellectual construct. The will cannot function as a logical construct. It is not an intellectual phenomenon. It emerges from the emotional depths of man. Estranged from its emotional origins the will becomes a useless intellectual ritual. It is this fragmentation of the self that made the client "helpless." The will did not fail the client, but rather the client failed his will. He protected himself from an encounter with the fear by emotional constriction. The constriction, in turn, cracked the self apart and disengaged the will. The tragic paradox is that the client made himself helpless by his own act. I will not argue that he was responsible for the fear, but he was responsible for the reaction he chose to it. He chose to be helpless rather than afraid.

The encounter cited above was a reversal of the decision to be afraid. Fear was no longer an isolated concept but a dreaded experience which penetrated the depths of his being. The encounter opened him to the existential terror of the fear. So did that same encounter open him to the existential dynamics of the self. The destructive process of self-estrangement initiated by the emotional constriction was reversed by the emotional impact of the encounter. The existential "risk" had made both the fear and the self which confronted that fear real. Now something could happen. There was an existent fear and an existent self to engage it. This was the breakthrough both the client and I knew was needed to precipitate a change. The intellectual stalemate ended. The struggle with existence began.

I find that innate potentials emerge when a client does risk his personal being. It is these potentials which enable him to survive the crisis. Primary among these emergent forces is the power of an effective will. The client discovers that he can choose and will his own reaction to any event in his life. It may be an event within his personal world such as the homosexual experience he described. So could it be an event in the external world such as a legal, political, or religious dogma. Now the client can choose and will his own reaction to any subjective event within himself as well as to any objective event in the external world which confronts him. He discovers in the pain of personal crisis that there are no restrictions on the power of his will—only those he makes for himself. He is as free as he chooses to be.

Such emergence of an effective will is one of the primary dynamics of the existential encounter. It can be experienced and comprehended. It cannot be reduced and explained. The will is an existential given. Freedom is inherent in the metaphysics of man.

I thus assert and argue that the existential encounter in psychotherapy makes freedom possible. So does it make freedom necessary at the same time. The critical encounter plunges the client into an existential moment below the depths of logical reduction. It tears him loose from the constricted boundaries of determinism. His reactions are no longer a function of psychosexual development, conditioned responses, or social pressures. Torn loose from such determinants he must find *within himself* the personal referent for his being. He must choose and will his own destiny. The same crisis that broke him free has forced him into an erect and solitary posture. Now he stands alone and must develop *from within* the self that he will be. He must forge *his own* being by *his own* choice and by *his own* will. The existential crisis which broke the yoke of determinism has burdened him with the labor of personal responsibility. Thus the experience which makes choice and will possible makes them necessary at the same time.

Nor does the labor of freedom end with the birth of will. Freedom is a constant struggle. It has no temporal dimension. Each moment it begins again. So it must be. The encounter which freed the client from historical determinism must free him from the history of his own choices as well. There is no temporal respite from the labor of freedom. Each moment of decision is a new challenge. Any decision determined by a prior choice would destroy the existential validity of that new decision. I remain free to choose and to will only as long as I remain open to the existential world which confronts me. Any closure to that world reverses the intrapsychic processes which make freedom possible. Yet the requirement for an open response does not preclude the possibility of personal commitment. It only demands that any such commitment be validated under the constant pressures of the existential moment. The labor of an open response to existence is the burden of freedom.

The emergence of an effective will is one metaphysical event in psychotherapy. I want to explore another metaphysical phenomenon which emerges from the same existential encounter. The will could be understood in relation to the client's dilemma: "I am helpless because I am afraid." The event which concerns me here must be understood in relation to his description of himself as "cut off from other people." He told me that when he saw someone cry he knew they must be in pain—still he could feel nothing for them. It was as if the other was a manikin with artificial tears. The emotional impact of the crying was smothered somewhere inside the cardboard form. His reaction to the lived world which confronted him was but a reflection of his own constricted self. The other was dead to him because he was dead to himself. The constriction which protected him from fear had dulled his response to pain as well. It was this emotional numbness which cut him off from himself and made him feel "cut off from other people." The isolation was due to this rupture of his relationship with himself. The interpersonal failure was not a function of social dynamics, but of *intra*psychic estrangement.

It is a paradox that my social being is not determined by my relationship to others, but by my relationship to myself. I can experience the world of the other only to the depth that I can experience my own subjective world. It was thus the disruption of the client's *intra*psychic processes which made him feel "cut off from other people." He felt estranged from others because fear had estranged him from himself. His whole emotional being had been deadened by the same constriction which isolated his fear. So did the reaction which killed the self wither its innate potentials. One of these innate potentials destroyed by the emotional constriction was the capacity for interpersonal communion.

The emergence of interpersonal communion is a metaphysical event. I cannot explain it. Logical operations cannot encompass it. Nevertheless, the experience itself is an almost *tangible* reality. It exists but defies conceptual closure. It forces me to a logical standstill. I can only describe the existential encounter which makes interpersonal communion possible. The crisis cited earlier is an example of such an encounter. The emotional impact of that crisis broke the abstract world of intellect into a concrete world of lived experience. The concept *fear* became a muffled shriek. *Pain* became a noxious ache. This metamorphosis of the client's lived world reflected an intrapsychic change. The world which confronted him was suddenly real because he was suddenly real to himself. The capacity for interpersonal communion emerges from such an intrapsychic change. The existential crisis which opens man to the inward experience of himself simultaneously opens him to the inward experience of the other. It is this emergence of an *interpersonal* existence which defies explanation. The mystery is "that because I can feel pain within myself I can feel pain within another." It does not follow logically. There is no causal link between his pain and mine. Nevertheless, the experience itself does follow. It leaps logical and causal necessity. Tears in the eyes of the other do flood my own heart. It is this interpersonal event which I cannot explain. Still the tears in my heart continue to flow in cogent testimony to it.

The existential encounter which generates metaphysical events can be understood. It is mundane. The fear and pain in our example are of this world. So do I argue that the events which emerge from such an encounter are inherent in the nature of man. Yet these metaphysical events are more difficult to grasp. Their origins are buried at depths which cannot be fathomed. Thus the emergence of interpersonal communion is like the emergence of will. It can be experienced and comprehended. It cannot be reduced and explained. The communion experience is an existential given. Love is inherent in the metaphysics of man.

I have tried to describe the emergence of freedom and love from the dynamics of the existential encounter. I set activation of these two human potentials as the goal for psychotherapy. They cannot be directly mobilized; they must be generated from the crisis of personal encounter. The client is estranged from these human resources because he is estranged from himself. The encounter integrates the fragmented self and restores the client to his natural intrapsychic state. It is the natural state of man because all his potential resources are now available to him. Freedom and love become vital expressions of his active being. He is no longer "helpless" and "cut off from other people." He has discovered himself and the metaphysics of the human condition.

My concentration on the encounter in psychotherapy has led me to recognize but one pathology and but one cure. The pathology is self-estrangement. The cure is self-encounter. So has this concentration led me to reject the significance of symptoms. It can be a nervous tick or a bizarre hallucination. It is all the same to me. These are but varied manifestations of intrapsychic estrangement. They are but varied reflections of fragmented selves. Thus there is no qualitative distinction between clients. They differ only in the degree of self-estrangement. Nor does this difference alter the one therapeutic goal of self-encounter. It affects only the difficulty of the therapeutic task. A therapist must exert greater strain on his own personal being to contact a more severely estranged client.

The encounter with the client is necessary, but it is not the primary goal. It only mediates the primary goal of the client's encounter with himself. The encounter with the therapist is necessary because it alters the client's intrapsychic structure. His interaction with himself has ossified into a closed defensive system. The dialogue with himself has become an abortive ritual. He must break that closed communication system to make contact with the therapist. The intrapsychic dynamics which open the client to this secondary encounter with the therapist simultaneously open him to the primary encounter with himself. The primary encounter then integrates the fragmented self and restores the natural intrapsychic state. It is restoration of the natural state which activates the innate potentials of the self. I have found these innate potentials to be constructive developmental forces. Constructive values emerge from the freedom to choose, and constructive relationships from the capacity to suffer the experience of another. The existential encounter which mobilizes these human resources is thus the fulcrum of the therapeutic process. Symptoms, values, social interaction, etc., are all contingent on it. The only problem in psychotherapy is self-estrangement. The only cure is self-encounter.

You may think that I have made too much over a brief moment in psychotherapy. Yet I consider such an existential encounter the crux of personality change and development. Its brevity can be no criterion for its significance. The breakthrough to existence cannot be evaluated by "the counting of words" or "the timing of responses." It must be evaluated by direct encounter with the dynamics of the intrapsychic crisis itself. I have tried to sketch my conception of these dynamics and their emergent metaphysics.

I have used the term *metaphysics* to refer to experiential events whose origins cannot be explained. So it is with freedom and love. I experience these events in the guts of my being. Still I cannot explain them. I can describe the emergence of these phenomena from the crisis of the existential encounter. Yet I can go no further. I cannot penetrate the mystery of their primary genesis.

It is true that freedom and love can be reduced to "illusions." It is then possible to explain their behavioral correlates. Yet "freedom" and "love" in a determined behavioral system are not the freedom and love that strain my existential guts. The verve and vigor of these emergent phenomena cannot be encompassed by logical operations. The immanence of existence is buried in the metaphysics of the human condition. I can testify to freedom and love, but I can go no further.

Yet the "professions" want to go further. They rush by existential man on their way to a systematic science of man. They trample the individual in their rush to more and more norms. They trample metaphysics in their rush to more and more data. They are in a hurry someplace. I do not know where. I only know it is not my way. I must remain behind. My commitment is to the concrete individual in his concrete struggle for freedom and for love. It may be too limited a goal for some. Still it is task enough for me. I do not seek to go further.

The Existential Ground

on existential mystery

Buber: I and Thou

That before which, in which, out of which, and into which we live, even the mystery, has remained what it was. It has become present to us and in its presentness has proclaimed itself to us . . . we have "known" it, but can acquire no knowledge from it which might lessen or moderate its mysteriousness. We have come near . . but not nearer to unveiling being or solving its riddle. We have felt release, but not discovered a "solution." We cannot approach others with what we have received, and say "you must do this, you must do this." We can only go, and confirm its truth. And this, too, is no "ought," but we can, we *must*.

Marcel: Being and Having

A problem is something which I meet, which I find complete before me, but which I can therefore lay siege to and reduce. But a mystery is something in which I myself am involved, and it can therefore only be thought of as 'a sphere where the distinction between what is in me and what is before me loses its meaning and its initial validity.' A genuine problem is subject to an appropriate technique by the exercise of which it is defined; whereas a mystery, by definition, transcends every conceivable technique. It is, no doubt, always possible (logically and psychologically) to degrade a mystery so as to turn it into a problem. But this is a fundamentally vicious proceeding, whose springs might perhaps be discovered in a kind of corruption of the intelligence.

Just because it is the essence of mystery to be recognized or capable of recognition, it may also be ignored and actively denied. It then becomes reduced to something I have "heard talked about" but which I refuse as only "being for other people"; and that, in virtue of an illusion which these "others" are deceived by, but which I myself claim to have detected.

on existential humanism

Camus: The Rebel

Then we understand that rebellion cannot exist without a strange form of love. Those who find no rest in God or in history are condemned to live for those who, like themselves, cannot live: in fact, for the humiliated. The most pure form of the movement of rebellion is thus crowned with the heart-rending cry . . . if all are not saved, what good is the salvation of one only? . . . This insane generosity is the generosity of rebellion, which unhesitatingly gives the strength of its love and without a moment's delay refuses injustice. Its merit lies in making no calculations, distributing everything it possesses to life and to living men. It is thus that it is prodigal in its gifts to men to come. Real generosity toward the future lies in giving all to the present.

Kierkegaard: The Concept of Dread

Only when the compassionate person is so related by his compassion
to the sufferer that in the strictest sense he comprehends that it is his
own cause which is here in question, only when he knows how to identify
himself in such a way with the sufferer that when he is fighting for an
explanation he is fighting for himself, renouncing all thoughtlessness,
softness, and cowardice, only then does compassion acquire significance
. . . generally . . . it is construed sentimentally and emotionally with
a cowardly sympathy which gives thanks to God for not being like such
a man, without comprehending that such an act of thanksgiving is
treason against God and against oneself, and without reflecting that
life has always in store analogous phenomena which perhaps one
will not escape. Sympathy one must have; but this sympathy is genuine
only when one knows oneself deeply and knows that what has happened
to one man may happen to all. Only thus can one be of some utility to
oneself and to others. The physician in an insane asylum who is foolish
enough to believe that he is wise for all eternity and that his bit of reason
is insured against all injury in life, is indeed in a certain sense wiser
than the crazy patients, but at the same time he is more foolish, and
he surely will not heal many.

Existential References

Berdyaev, Nicolas
  The Meaning of the Creative Act. Translated by Donald A. Lowrie.
  New York: Collier Books, 1962. P. 134.
  Slavery and Freedom. Translated by R. M. French. New York: Scribner's,
  1944. Pp. 21, 22.
  Solitude and Society. Passage cited translated by Donald A. Lowrie
  from the original Russian. 1934. P. 102.

Buber, Martin
  Between Man and Man. Translated by Ronald G. Smith with Afterword
  by the Author and Introduction by Maurice Friedman. New York:
  Macmillan, 1965. P. 97.
  I and Thou. Translated by Ronald G. Smith. (2nd end.) with Postscript
  by the Author. New York: Scribner's, 1958. P. 111.

Camus, Albert
  The Myth of Sisyphus, and Other Essays. Translated by Justin O'Brien.
  New York: Vintage, 1960. P. 88.
  The Rebel. An Essay on Man in Revolt. Translated by Anthony Bower.
  New York: Vintage, 1956. Pp. 283, 304.

Dostoevsky, Fyodor
  Notes from the Underground. Translated by Constance Garnett. New
  York: Dell, 1960. Pp.34, 46, 50.

Kierkegaard, Sören
  The Concept of Dread. Translated with Introduction by Walter Lowrie.
  Princeton: Princeton University Press, 1957. Pp. 48, 49, 107.
  Concluding Unscientific Postscript. Translated by David F. Swenson;
  completed with Introduction and Notes by Walter Lowrie. Princeton:
  Princeton University Press, 1941. Pp. 68f, 109, 115, 165, 182, 373, 437.

Marcel, Gabriel
  Being and Having: An Existentialist Diary. New York: Harper & Row,
  1965. P. 117.

Sartre, Jean-Paul
  The Emotions. Outline of a Theory. Translated by Bernard Frechtman.
  New York: Philosophical Library, 1948. P. 4.